Dedicated to those who lost their life to mental health illness
and to those who are at war with their mind,
stay strong.

In Loving Memory of Alice

AT WAR WITH MY MIND

by

Rachael Hollwey

ISBN 9798370928949

Cover photography by Babanov Photography

PROLOGUE

Home and School Life

I am the youngest of three girls and I had a great childhood with my sisters and the most loving parents.

There are so many memories from all the Christmases and birthdays together, the playing and the fighting, the laughter and the tears. I miss those days.

We were very fortunate to go on adventurous holidays, camping in France and road trips around Europe, Florida and the Caribbean.

It is thanks to my loving family that I am here telling this story today. Because, contrary to my life at home, my school days were hard as I was bullied by various people. Since it was never in physical form but rather mentally it was not seen by others. This is also why I did not think anyone would easily believe me and I decided to remain silent. The latter attitude was later motivated also by the fact that the bullying occurred by different people and in different occasions – I began to think it could be my fault!

I strove to remain vibrant, always smiling and focusing on the positive aspects of my life to help cope and I managed to enjoy many good memories and still thrived in school.

Until an episode of hypoxia, starvation of oxygen to the brain, changed my life forever. I remember my temperature fluctuating so rapidly and going from extremes of hot and cold – I still have visions of not being able to breath and sometimes feel this as a physical memory. It took hours to begin recovering and then I remember someone holding my hands, helping me to walk and having to direct me to move my legs saying, "left, right, left, right." Some said later this helped reconnect my brain and the after effects might have been even more traumatic without it.

This event was life changing. The neuropathways of my brain had been altered, triggering the start of my suffering from Anorexia Nervosa and depression.

In the days that followed, my body began to reject food and I drastically lost weight.

This made people care for me with concern. In this new condition, my brain made the connection that if I looked physically unwell, the silence of the suffering would be broken as, not being able to do it verbally, my body would speak out for me and stop the bullying. My mind simply rejected food as to keep it this way.

Everything written comes direct from the diaries I kept throughout the years of battling mental illness. It is the raw truth of what the demons in my mind were telling me and what they did to me.

Mental illness manifests in many ways and various treatments work differently for each individual. Those I underwent that we unable to help me, may be beneficial to others.

Some people may find parts of this book traumatic, but its purpose is to create an understanding for carers, professionals and suffers alike, and to give hope that recovery can be found from the darkest of places.

1

The beginning: Diagnosis of Anorexia Nervosa

I was fourteen years old when I begged my parents to let me go on a ski trip with the school. I had always left out having been severely bullied in junior school and enduring this again in senior school. This time I finally had friends as well and I had to do anything to keep it that way and make life bearable.

My Mum regrets ever allowing me to go, but no-one could have predicted what would happen and assure her never to blame herself.

The bullying continued on this trip, though I desperately tried to join in and be just like everyone else, having fun with friends. But a severe panic attack and trauma caused me to suffer from hypoxia, starvation of oxygen to the brain.

The teachers were on the phone to the doctors and my parents while trying to get me to breathe in rhythm, to stabilise my temperature as I fluctuated between overheating to ice cold in quick succession. I could not move, I felt paralysed. It took hours before I began to come around, I had pins and needles down my arms and I could not coordinate my mind or my body, I remember someone holding my hands to tell me how to walk by moving my feet, "right, left, right, left".

It was the penultimate evening, and I was not allowed to ski on the final day. I sat with the teachers alternating to be with me, trying to get me to eat and drink but I could not eat for a few days with my body rejecting it, this resulted in weight loss and looking physically unwell. The journey home was a blur, physically and emotionally weakened.

We believe the hypoxia caused my brain chemistry to be altered, and my Dad found research on this later in my illness when desperate to find a cure for me, this ultimately being what saved me in the end. But suddenly everyone seemed to care about me, teachers and friends were concerned and looking after me and the bullying stopped. So, with my brain chemistry already altered, I believe this then took it further with my brain connecting looking ill with being cared for. New neuropath ways were forming and becoming more engrained with this association, so that it became that I *would not* eat, or was not allowed to eat.

At this stage, no-one considered the possibility that my brain and mentality had been severely impacted. Naturally we all thought I would simply recover from the hypoxia. Over the next two years my physical and mental well-being gradually declined, but it was not noticeable enough to be of concern to anyone, and it was put down to normal adolescent changes. Until one night when I woke up with a jolt of panic and anxiety, I do not know why, but I suddenly knew something was wrong and that I was suffering from Anorexia Nervosa.

It is rare in this illness to self-diagnose, but I have always been a slightly different case throughout.

First thing in the morning I picked up the phone to call the doctor. I was incredibly anxious and kept hanging up when there was an answer. Eventually I got that extra bit of courage to make an appointment.

I told my doctor I thought I was suffering from anorexia, I was so relieved that I had said it, could now get help, and begin to recover.

I wish it had been that easy.

My doctor told me my BMI was not that low. BMI is a measurement of Body Mass Index to indicate if a person is within the correct weight category for their height. The healthy range is said to be between 18.5 and 24.9, but is not an adequate indicator of health and I do not believe it should be used. However, my BMI was still below the healthy range at sixteen, yet the doctor told me it was just a phase I was going through. She went through the motions and did a generic assessment of questions, ticked the boxes, and I left.

"You're BMI is not that low", was a pinnacle moment. I needed help and wanted help, but for that I felt I now had to lose more weight.

I was going on holiday with my friend and her family the following week and the doctor said that a nice break away should sort it. Simple.

The guilt still looms over me from that holiday. I rapidly deteriorated and my friend had to helplessly watch that. I would not eat much, I did not have any energy and I was constantly anxious. I had to borrow clothes from her younger cousin as mine were becoming too big.

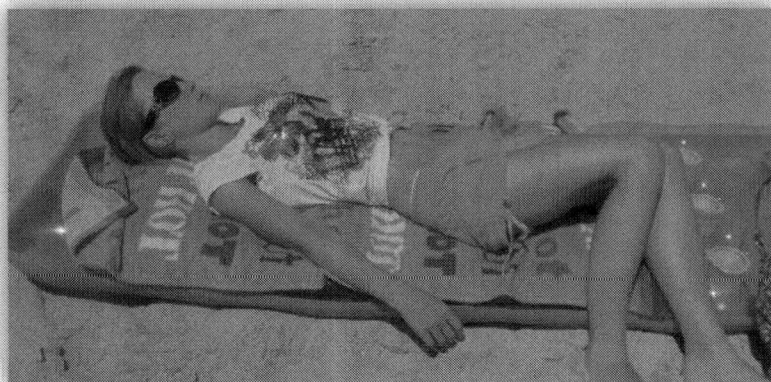

In the photos from that holiday my eyes were lifeless, and the smiles were forced. Throughout my illness people said they knew I was "Rex" was in control of my mind when my eyes had no life or sparkle in them.

When I was home from this holiday, I went back to the doctor for the routine follow-up appointment. When she weighed me again, I had lost a lot of weight in just two weeks. She looked at me in shock and immediately referred me for help.

A little too late. Anorexia had a firm grip on me now, it was deeper than I even knew.

My life suddenly went from making plans with friends and career goals, to making meal plans and weight goals.

I went to the Children's Mental Health ward weekly with my Mum. They did my blood pressure and my weight, noted that both were lower each time, and then sent me on my way.

I was nearly eighteen years old, but on paper this is still not classified as an adult so I had to attend the children's services. However, because I was close to being an adult and I would have to change services soon, they were not able to give me a full programme to begin a recovery plan and just measured the decline in my physical health each week.

The early stages are crucial, especially when I was so determined and willing to get better. I had been turned away on the first day I asked for help, causing me to go deeper into the illness. Now I had a few more months of limited help because of my age and "Rex" took over my mind a little more each day.

"Rex" began to tell me that it was because I deserved to suffer and I did not deserve the help to get better. That feeling of not deserving anything and needing punishment continued to escalate through my illness with it possibly stemming from here.

It got to the point that I kept myself awake day and night for as long as I could because I did not think I deserved to sleep. It was torture.

When I was finally able to start appointments with the Adult Eating Disorder service, they said the situation of having to start in the Children's services was a mistake, that it should not have happened and will not again. I am pleased I could help stop this happening to others, but it caused me a lot of damage.

This seemed to keep happening to me throughout. Mistakes being made with me and then learnt from for others. I love to help people, it is a big part of my personality, but it was always at jeopardy of myself. Thankfully another part of my personality is determination and rising to challenges. I would never give up.

I was at war so I created an army. My family and friends were the strongest support network I could have ever ask for and they stood right by my side to give me the strength to battle on the front line; I wanted to win, I really and truly did. But each time I was being shot down and becoming weaker.

I had a constant argument in my head between Rachael and "Rex". Even at night I would have a dream that I had eaten something unhealthy, and I would wake up in such a state of anxiety. When I realised it was a dream, the relief was indescribable. Usually this feeling comes to people if they had a dream about a loved one or a real tragedy.

I did everything I could to beat the voice, coming up with ammunition to tell myself why I needed to eat, why I needed to gain weight, that I was not disgusting. I read quotes to stay positive and made analogies to better understand what I was going through. I kept talking to my army of people about what was going on in my mind and would try to distract myself by playing games and starting to draw. But I had an invader in my mind and no matter what I did, "Rex" kept winning. It was powerful.

It was exhausting.

Anorexia becomes a game of deception and tricks, lying to the ones you love. I hated this and deep down it hurt. My actions felt involuntary and as though I had no control over them.

At breakfast, I would quickly put water on my cereal from my glass, and then add a splash of milk for the colour. Delicious. I would cut out the middle of a bread roll, so it would still look like a whole one, and no-one would know.

I would take a biscuit, throw most of it away, and wait until someone walked in and then eat the tiny bit I had, to make it look like I had eaten a whole biscuit.

My heart would race as dinner was served, to get that fraction of a second to put a potato on someone else's plate.

When I prepared food for myself and others, I would cook theirs "properly", with things like butter and oil so that they would think I was eating that too. I had skipped these elements with my own food. Each time I was successful in deception, I would not feel relieved or calm, I would feel I had to do better next time.

"Rex" would also deceive me. I could not see that I was physically unwell. In fact, the more weight I lost, the bigger I saw myself. You may have seen pictures where someone underweight is in front of the mirror and the reflection is obese.

This is genuinely what you see and is another sign of this illness being to do with the brain and neuropath ways. Someone telling me I was not fat was like me trying to convince you the world is indeed flat.

I knew how awful I had felt by looking at my reflection in a window but had the compulsion to constantly check.

My mum bought wallpaper to stick over my mirrors to help stop this but seeing my reflection in the doors either side was enough to be just as painful.

My sister once caught me looking at my legs and saw my distress. She said to me "don't worry, I've seen worse". This caused such anxiety as she could see I was fat as well. I knew everyone else was lying! However, she meant she had seen thinner, thinking I was distressed because I was so thin.

I made the family home became a house of tension and uncertainty. No-one knew how, or who, I would be from one minute to the next. They were walking on a minefield with everything they said and did causing an explosion.

The people around me were becoming the enemy and "Rex" was my best friend.

Everyday tasks became stressful events.

I would go food shopping with my Dad, it was too much for my Mum seeing the agony during this strenuous task and I definitely could not manage on my own. We would have to allocate a couple of hours so that we could go and analyse all the food, talk about it, and go backwards and forwards as I tried to decide what to buy through the arguments between "Rachael" and "Rex".

If I had a meal out at a restaurant, I would analyse the menu from a week before, search for pictures of each meal and try to decide what I could have. When at the restaurant, I could not engage in the conversation, I would be thinking about what they could be doing to my food in the kitchen and focusing on breathing so that I did not have a panic attack. When the food came, I would be arguing in my mind the whole time as to whether it was safe or not, how much to eat, and if I had to be punished for it later.

I had a weekend away with my Dad in Ireland to try and help me. The most ideal trip for me with it being my favourite place and having quality daddy-daughter time. But it was taken over by the thoughts of food and exercise, filled with anxiety and stress.

It is tradition that my Grandad would get us a Chinese takeaway on the night we arrived, this brought him so much joy, but would bring me such despair. I debated about this for a month leading up to the trip! When Grandad made that offer, my Dad started saying "no not this time…". I looked at my Granddad's confusion, I could not do this to him. I jumped in saying "yes, yes we will". The joy on my Dad's face as well as my Granddad's would make the suffering worth it. I compromised with Dad to allow us to walk to get it, and I also went for very plain and healthy options. It was still a positive step and made for a nice evening.

In my diary on this trip, I had written about food again. Not what we did, not the time together, the food. I freaked out at lunch because of the amount of sauce on it and it ruined the whole day. It was 10 years ago, but I can still remember the exact lunch and the way I felt. The feelings are so traumatic, they leave a scar.

Dad took me to visit Grandma's grave and I was thinking how she would have given me the best Grandma hug you could imagine and I knew she would have just made it a little easier somehow. I longed for her to be back. But she still helped me and gave me some strength back to continue through that day. Little did I know just how much she would still help me later.

I desperately tried to keep a normal life of socialising, working and studying.

I had push myself to go out with my friends, as each time I missed out, I felt one step further away from them all and one step closer to "Rex".

But joining in soon had a worse effect. I would be so cold, unable to stand up for too long, stressing over the calories in the drinks and feeling self-conscious in any outfit. Sometime feeling too thin, sometimes feeling too fat. By going to the parties, people saw how much I had changed and I was not really present with the distraction of my mind. People would be concerned with how unwell I was becoming each time. It was a no-win situation whether I went or not and eventually I was no longer invited.

I do not even remember some events I went to. I was so consumed by the illness at the time.

In my diary, I was describing the stress of going to a concert with my family. I assumed it was to see "Pink" as I went a few times and remember this but when it said we had been to see Guns 'n' Roses, I was in shock and I had to ask my parents if I had got this right. Yes. We had travelled to Birmingham and had seen Guns 'n' Roses live, an event of a lifetime. I cannot recall it, not at all, not even a little bit.

This was incredibly upsetting for me. The only thing that helped, was that I seem to follow in my Dad's footsteps in life, and he too had seen Guns 'n' Roses live without knowing it!

My parents were invited along to the first flight with Virgin Atlantic to Australia, by and with Richard Branson. On the last night, Guns 'n' Roses were playing, my Dad's favourite band. They had not slept, and had partied constantly, so he merely said, "I like this song, they are good". Only upon return, when "Sweet Child O' Mine" came on the radio, did he realise he was in the presence of Guns 'n' Roses

for a private concert!

I just wish my memory lapse was because of too much partying, and not possession.

My 18th birthday did not involve this level of partying either. I had a slumber party with make your own pizzas and games like hide and seek. As if I was turning six years old.

My personality remains that of a child to this day, but for fun and laughter in between moments of business and adult life, but not for my 18th birthday.

I still spent most of the time in the kitchen cleaning, because having fourteen friends over and food around was so incredibly stressful for me. I was so tired, I had been doing exercise in the garden and in my room at every opportunity through the day to be able to have pizza and champagne in the evening.

My friends and family were so supportive to do this for me and get involved to ensure I did get a celebration on my 18th.

So now I was 18 and had a new world to explore! I was an adult, I could go out clubbing, go to university and have more freedom in life! But I had a whole different world ready for me with a lot less freedom.

When I managed to go clubbing, I would dance a lot, not because I was happy and having fun, but to burn calories. I would not be able to eat the next day because of the regret of how many calories were in the drinks. I would have a hangover like everyone, but not be able to stay in bed, I had to keep on the move. Next time you get back at 4am having had shots of tequila, get up at 8am, do not eat anything, and do not sit down until 9pm... torture!

Friends also began to go on holiday together, as opposed to with family. An exciting time for many.

Each year a group of my friends went to a Centre Parcs, a holiday resort, for a week away, but this was too much for me so I always went to join for just one day. I still brought my own food

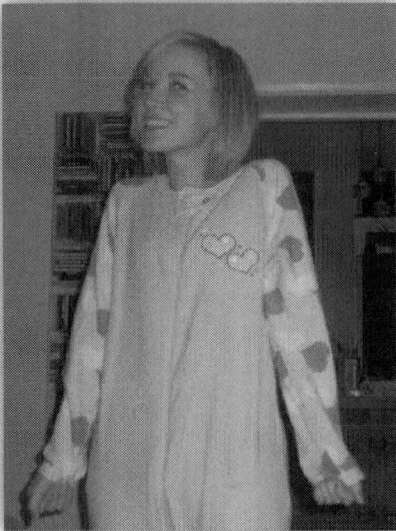

and I ate at the times I was allowed to, as opposed to when everyone else was. I had to wear a t-shirt and shorts in the swimming pool so as to not upset my friends and could not go on the slides because it hurt my spine too much with being skeletal.

Not even one day of freedom, could you not have allowed me just one day?

I got the courage to go on a weekend away for a friend's birthday. A lodge in a forest with a jacuzzi, beautiful scenery and just time away to play games, eat food and enjoy a few drinks. That was the idea. They soon realised the reality of my illness.

Again, I brought my own food. I would exercise in my room before leaving the lodge, walk all day long, leave the room when food came out, and just caused a huge amount of stress on my friends who watched the agony with no means of helping me, much like my parents felt at home. The guilt still looms over my head at how much I ruined that holiday.

I also went away with my sister on a houseboat with a youth group and amongst incredibly supportive, positive people. I know my sister found my illness hard, so it was an honour that she had invited me. She was incredibly supportive and allowed me to bring some of my own food but said she would help me if I wanted to try things they were having. This showed me how much she understood that it was sheer torture in my head, and not just "a silly phase".

The first evening we were sat in a circle while people played acoustic guitar, prayed and were just so happy. I cannot tell you how powerful this was, I could not hold back the tears and began to cry, possibly for the first time since I was diagnosed. My sister put her arm around me and cried with me. What this meant to me, I can never describe.

I was working two jobs and at one point I was working six. I was trying to study at college and had regular appointments at the hospital. In the school/college holidays I worked for 8 hours as a children's

entertainer at a leisure centre followed by an evening shift at the local theatre. I also had exams looming and was trying to study for these. The stress of juggling all of this would have been a lot for anyone, add on battling anorexia, and you are not going to manage for long.

But I had to keep busy at every moment, a pause meant I could hear the voice. I also held hope that I would eventually beat this and have a future, so I needed an education. I wanted to save money in case I did end up in hospital, so that I had something ready when I came back out.

I know people may think my family should have simply stopped me from doing so much. But as I say, it is a clever illness and I managed to twist it into being positive. I was also now 18, they had no real power over me. All they could do was watch and wait.

Everyone was suffering. My Dad said, "It is surreal to look at you, it is like looking in one of those funhouse mirrors where it makes you look really thin. I'm having to watch my baby daughter waste away in front of my eyes".

My Mum was having nightmares about choosing my coffin. She stayed strong and was firm with me to help me fight "Rex" but would also hug me close and say she loves me. I would see her cry when she thought I was not there. I could see she was heading for a breakdown. My sisters were trying to understand and would question me a lot. They would then get the wrath of "Rex" as if they were intruding. They were not allowed to know too much.

Friends were beginning to distance themselves, telling me they could not handle watching me become so ill and be taken over when I was such a strong and energetic person before. A friend told me it was not enjoyable to be with me anymore, that she felt responsible for me and like my therapist. It is no wonder I was not invited to days out anymore.

We were all powerless, in turmoil and did not know what to do. No-one did.

There were still a few glimmers of hope which would be so unexpected and sudden, as if my brain flickered back to normal. I remember when we went out for a meal for Mother's Day and I found the meal difficult. Understandably, when desserts were ordered I was not offered any, my sisters and parents asked for a dessert to share between them. I felt so ashamed and isolated that I was not included, so I got a sudden surge of courage to shock everyone and ordered one for myself!

"Apple Sponge Tart please."

My family were stunned, we did not' mention it while we waited in case we rocked the boat or woke "Rex" up! When it came, I enjoyed it as if there were nothing wrong, it made everyone so happy, they actually clapped when I finished! This is how bad things had gotten. Though these moments were such a relief to all, they were few and far between and ultimately not enough to stop the decline.

I felt both guilty and ashamed to keep using my friends and family to tell them the dark thoughts in my mind. But I did not want to stay quiet, that is what "Rex" wanted. I was always desperately trying to find a way out of this.

I started using external help. If I were struggling, I would be able to login to "B-eat", an online support network for eating disorders. I admire these foundations for the work they do, and later on in my illness, they were lifesaving.

I attended a support group where I met another girl who was in a similar situation to me. This was invaluable to have someone who truly understood. We became a team and battled together.

The first time we met up, we went out for a meal and ordered challenging food. We could enjoy it and do it together, it felt safer. When the waiter collected our empty plates, he commented that we now probably would not eat for a week, as we were so thin so we could not possibly eat well. We looked at each other and ordered a dessert and finished the whole of that as well to make our point! I have experienced these types of comments throughout, whether in a restaurant or on the streets. It is beyond me as to why this seems acceptable to people.

I remember that exact meal. Seabass with mashed potato and a creamy sauce, followed by crème brulee and shortbread biscuits. It was rare to have an enjoyable meal, and this was the first in a long time which is why I can remember it so well.

We kept this up for a while, we were doing really well. But in the vicious world of anorexia, the more you fight, the more "Rex" fights. We were not strong enough as a team anymore, we would put on a brave face together, but were struggling behind the scenes. This friendship soon became more hostile with our illness taking over and making it competitive.

It is one of the only illnesses that you become driven to be WORSE than others. A patient with cancer would not be envious if someone else's had spread further. You would not be jealous if someone had lifelong injuries after an accident and your injuries could be treated.

It is something that is hard for anyone to understand. It may be to stop you forming this teamwork, to stop you having someone else to fight with and to keep you alone. It may be to entice you into becoming more ill, thus be in the tighter grip of "Rex".

The charities and volunteer groups were saviours. They are incredible people.

There was a walk-in centre near my house, where you could go night and day to talk to a support worker. Knowing this was here was such a safety net. If I could not cope, they were there to listen, let me break down, scream and help rationalise the thoughts in my mind. I did not have to constantly lean on my family and friends, I would use my strength to hold it together in front of them and then go to the centre on my way home to let out the agony.

In the beginning these schemes helped to calm my mind and continue on through the day, but they soon became the saviours of my life.

All I wanted was the simple pleasures in life that I use to enjoy. "Rex" took anything and everything from you. In particular family time. We no longer sat at the table for dinner together, it was not a nice experience anymore. We used to play games, at least all sit in the same room, but we were all becoming distant. Partially because of the natural way this now happens in people's busy lives, but I knew I was a big part to play.

Christmas was a significant sign of this. I was, and still am, a fanatic about Christmas. The joy, the time spent together, the food… needless to say, not even this day brought joy anymore.

I would need a meticulous food plan to follow for each meal, and even snacks – by which I mean, allowing two chocolates in the day, and two crackers with a sprinkle of cheese if I were lucky.

I remember the first Christmas with anorexia. I was anxious from the very beginning when I forgot to put Bucks Fizz into my meal plan, so I would not allow myself to have it. I made breakfast which meant my bagel had no butter, some of the bread cut off, a slither of salmon and a spoon of egg. That would have to keep me going until dinner at 3 or 4pm. Possibly one chocolate in between.

I had new potatoes instead of roast and my own instant gravy made with water. I could have one slice of turkey and ham, boiled vegetables only, and one bite of a pig in blanket. The pig in blanket showed to be too much, and I did not manage this. This upset my sister as it used to be our "thing", we loved those so much and would eat three or four, racing each other to the last one!

I promised my mum all week that if she allowed me to have my own food at dinner, I would have a mince pie in the evening. When it came to it, I could not. This triggered a lot of anger, a lot of tears. We shouted and screamed. I hated it. I hated conflict. I hated hurting my family.

Rachael desperately wanted to eat the mince pie to stop it all, seemingly such a simple solution, but "Rex" was so strong, I can never explain what it is really like, but believe me when I say, it would have been a lot worse if I had eaten it.

The silver lining to this was that Mum and Dad saw the raw truth to what was happening. I told them that I had a voice in my head and of the turmoil I felt I had to lose weight to get help, but had to look as though I was doing well around them as to not hurt or disappoint them.

They were shocked to hear it and were sorry I had not been able to tell them sooner. They were now more determined than ever to get me help.

I was becoming very weak. I was so cold it was agonising, and I was suffering from insomnia, which meant I did not even get a rest from my mind at night. I felt so unwell from hunger, faint and short of breath. Sometimes when I went to bed, I felt like my body was giving up, which did install fear into me and so I would literally crawl downstairs to the kitchen and get a small bowl of cereal. This showed that somewhere, deep down, I did not want to die yet.

The outpatient system was not as supportive as I had hoped. The doctor I was seeing constantly changed, which meant I had to keep going through the motions of my BMI, where it all began, my work and family life and so on. Sometimes I would go four weeks between appointments, and I did not seem to receive any real therapy. They would say that I needed to be a higher weight to do therapy. But I felt I needed therapeutic help to gain weight.

Being home without professional support was becoming scary. Things were spiralling downhill and I could not combat my own mind for much longer.

I was now fearful of every element in food.

I had a bowl of soup and went into panic about the high levels of salt in it, so I looked up if this would make me gain weight and found it retained water temporarily. Advice was to drink a litre of water to flush it out of your system, so that is what I did straight away. When I was having breathing difficulties, I thought it was due to the salt content of what I had eaten. The possibility of it being the strain on my heart from malnourishment never crossed my mind.

I could not use tomato ketchup or salad cream because of the extra calories. I could not go out to eat any more, even if I did examine the menu and the photos.

My gums were blistered and bleeding from diet carbonated drinks to keep me full.

I had to plan my weeks food in full with great analysis. It made eating near impossible as nothing was "right".

How long could this go on for?

The outpatients team kept pushing another treatment they have, called "Day Care". Yes, day care.

When I was waiting for my appointments, I would see the day care patients together, laughing and smiling, walking around in slippers and looking very comfortable. Sometimes I did want to be amongst them and go through it with others.

I debated in my mind what was best to do. I would have to leave college, a huge detriment to my future, but I could not even concentrate at college anymore, could not retain the information with the malnourishment. At this rate I would not live to see a future anyway, so I made the decision to go into the day-care programme.

Then I was told it was currently full and I would go on the waiting list.

I had accepted in my mind that I needed more intensive care, and now I was told I could not have it. This took me another step further into the darkness. I had surrendered, I had succumbed to giving up "real" life and being well and truly in the world of eating disorders. So now that is where I felt I belonged, and my thoughts were slowly changing to not wanting to leave this life, it had become my reality for so long, I did not know how to live a life without it.

The waiting game began, the first of what would be many. Waiting for the call to say there is a bed or space in hospital for you is horrific. You give up the exhausting fight somewhat and just do the bare minimum. You have tried so hard, used a lot of energy, and now know there is no chance of winning until in intensive care. The demons in your head are angry and go into full attack to make you as ill as possible before going in. Many lose their lives at this point; I was nearly one of them.

2

Life of a Day Patient

The night before my first day at the unit "Rex" was angry and attacking my mind with all its strength. I did not belong there, I was not ill enough, I did not deserve to have that space. But the next morning I rang the bell to the door and stepped through into my new world, and it was not a nice one.

It was like being caught in a time-lapse of walking into the small lounge each morning with 11 other patients, taking my designated seat on the sofa for the day and desperately finding ways to distract my mind or just curling up under a blanket to hide from my new reality. On a Monday and Thursday morning, there was the agonising wait to be called in to be weighed - gain weight and you have a bigger fight with the demons all day, lose weight and you are in trouble with the staff. Walking back into the lounge afterwards, the other patients look over to try and judge your demeanour and work out if you had lost or gained weight. The ever-competitive illness.

I would look at the timetable for what groups were on that day, not that I needed to as I had learnt it fairly quickly; psychotherapy, body image, nutrition, mindfulness. It sounded holistic and helpful, but they would just go through a course from a textbook on repeat. I should have been running between a biology lab and sports hall with an intense timetable for my A-levels, not walking up and down a small corridor in my pyjama socks to either eat or be told how much I was ruining my life in the "therapy" groups.

I remember a time when we were made to spell our names using playdoh. That was the group. I still do not know how that helped me either. It made me feel patronised and ashamed.

Lounge, dining room, group. Lounge, dining room, group. Lounge, dining room, group. Then home for an evening of torture from the demons in my head until walking back into the lounge the next morning.

I was the youngest patient there with the age range from eighteen to sixty. Majority had already been in the day hospital once, twice or multiple times as well as other inpatient units. It made me realise that this illness will stay with you for life if you allow it to, that I could go through this torture every day for the rest of my life. It was an incentive, but I was also worried that it could happen to me.

To keep myself fighting, I became determined to be a role model and show people that it does not have to be this way, that it can be beaten the first time! I made a good friend in this unit who had the same attitude and determination, so we stuck together and helped each other through it. We are still good friends to this day.

At the beginning of the admission, I was on a smaller meal plan and slowly built up to the full plan to avoid "re-feeding syndrome" which can be dangerous. This occurs when someone has been severely restricting food and when it is reintroduced, it can cause electrolyte imbalance and other complications. At the meals I saw what the others had and I was in fear that I would have to eat that amount soon, it made me start hoping my weekly blood tests had abnormalities so that they could not increase my diet.

We sat around the table in the supervised dining room – patients nearing the end of admission were in an unsupervised dining room - and went up one by one to the food trolley. For breakfast we used a mug to measure a portion of cornflakes, having to make it exactly to the top and sometimes being made to add three or four more cornflakes to fill the spaces. Then crouching down to measure the milk in a jug so slowly to precisely 200ml –" Rex" would not allow it a millilitre above and the staff would not allow it a millilitre below.

Sitting back down with the cereal with the other patients and members of staff who now have the task of pouring orange juice to the exact line on the glass.

When finally starting to eat breakfast, the staff would watch very carefully so you do not deceive them in anyway and manage to get rid of some of the food.

When on the full diet, you then go to the kitchen to meet another member of staff, take two slices of bread and toast it. What a simple task. Not for us. We would subtly analyse the loaf of bread, reaching down for the thinnest slices. I remember everyone being called for a meeting about this, how it had to stop, and we debated this issue for over an hour.

Taking your toast back around the corner to the dining room, being watched of course, and pick a pot of butter and jam. Spreading time. Having to get into every corner and not leave a spec as the pots were then inspected by the staff. Being incredibly careful not to make too many crumbs while eating the toast or you would have to scoop them up and eat them.

When everyone had successfully completed the mission of breakfast, we would go back through to the lounge with staff and have "food and feelings", where we would talk for an hour about how the meal went. Often very argumentative of "he did this, she did that". Sometimes silence with everyone feeling traumatised by the food.

This was the same system for lunchtime. Waiting in agony to go to the trolley and see what the torturous food looked like and take your carefully measured portion.

After the main meal, we would repeat the system to get dessert. I can only describe it as "hospital food" and often full of oil and cheese. Meals being things such as pies, lasagnes, quiche, macaroni cheese, fish and chips and desserts being apple pie, fruit crumble, treacle tart – oh I remember that treacle tart so well. Ready-made pastry case filled with pure sugar and sticky golden syrup. My teeth hurt eating it, still the most sickly and difficult dessert I have come across to this day! All desserts came with two scoops of ice cream or a full ladle of custard.

When everyone had finished, we then returned to the lounge to talk about the meal.

Once a week we would have "breakfast challenge" and "sandwich challenge". For breakfast we had things like two croissants, yoghurt, fruit and juice or large bacon rolls, buttered with four slices of bacon, fruit and juice.

For the sandwiches, we would make our own! It is hard for me to even believe how much turmoil this caused. We were challenged to cut our own bread from a bakery loaf and I would be shaking as I was terrified to cut it too thick, if it was thicker than everyone else's I would make "Rex" angry. We had to weigh out the filling, which is not promoting normality with food, and it was usually cheese, a lot of cheese. I would be in floods of tears. Making my own food was as though I was giving myself permission and it was more *my* fault for eating.

In between these meals, snacks would be brought in on a tray to the lounge.

Just 1 hour after breakfast we had milk and biscuits. However sometimes, we were given a surprise "snack challenge" where the tray would have a chocolate bar, cake or some other form of torture on it. The panic, anxiety and fear was incredibly high from each of us. Imagine being locked inside a room with your worst fear being inflicted of you with no means to escape.

There was a particular time, one month into my admission where we were told it would be carrot cake the next day for "snack challenge". Following that was fish and chips for lunch and sticky toffee pudding for dessert. To any ordinary person this was a lot for one day and quite unhealthy, let alone for someone with an eating disorder and all before 1pm.

I was in panic all evening and in the morning, I phoned in sick to the unit. Of course they did not believe me, so therefore knew I was very distressed, but failed to help either. They tormented me with merely saying, "don't worry, we will save the nicest looking slice for you tomorrow instead", with a note of humour in their voice. I dropped the phone down in hysterical tears. Being such a "people pleaser" I was also worrying that they now hated me as well as still having to have the cake. I was in turmoil.

I ended up going to the unit that day, I remember cutting the cake and shaking like someone had a gun to my head. I would not talk and my key worker said, "if Rachael does not talk, I'm going to get angry". I snapped back at her. I am not a child *or* a prisoner.

I ate the cake. I ate the fish and chips. I ate the sticky toffee pudding. I ran from the unit before the 3:30pm snack of a build-up shake and was then tortured to exercise until I nearly collapsed and not be allowed to eat anything else for the rest of the day.

We had another snack two hours after lunch before leaving the unit at 3:30pm. This was either a fort sip (build up milkshake), a chocolate bar or crisps depending on your meal plan.

Then it was home time.

Help me.

It is going to get me. Torture me. Punish me. I cannot cope.

You are expected to go home and simply continue on with the day. I was given a meal plan for dinner, another dessert and another snack. That was not going to happen.

My head was a mess at home. I had sat in a lounge all day, eaten a large amount of food by anyone's standards and had infuriated the demons who were there ready for me when I left the unit. As much as I hated being there, I dreaded leaving the door.

Think of when you have indulged at a Christmas dinner, how tired you feel and cannot even think of eating anymore. I was incredibly full from food that was not the most nutritious and had battled my own mind all day... I was exhausted! And now I had to manage from 4pm until the next morning, by which I mean obey the demons and exercise to excess and avoid eating anything for the rest of the day. I lived with my parents so I had to be clever to do this, seizing the opportunity to put sauce on a plate and making it seem used, not be seen for half an hour and pretend I had eaten dinner along with many other tricks.

Needless to say, I was not a nice person to be around. I was incredibly depressed, angry and anxious.

It became a horrible game. When I was in the unit I would have to cope with the incredibly high diet while sitting and doing nothing, and when I was on my own in the evening and weekends, I would eat the absolute minimum that I could and push my body to exhaustion with exercise. Why? I was missing out on college being at the unit and putting myself through a living nightmare, what was the point if I was balancing it out with these detrimental actions?

I still cannot answer this. All I can say again, is it is powerful. More powerful than you could ever imagine.

I remember the terrifying feeling of how little control I had over myself. When I started exercising in the house, I would be praying for someone to return home so that I could stop. Feeling exhausted, weak and physically sick was not enough.

I have a vivid vision from when I went out into my garden on the trampoline, to bounce and exercise as much as I could. The screaming in my head was so loud, my body was so tired, but I kept going and going until my legs gave way and I could not physically bounce any more. I curled up in the middle of my trampoline under my coat, hiding, hiding from the torture. Screaming, "stop", "make it go away". The neighbours must have wondered what on earth was going on!

I do not know how long I was out there. When my Dad came home and realised I was there, he came over and I can just remember tears and shouting random thoughts of torment that did not make sense. I cannot even imagine what that moment was like for my Dad.

I was becoming more and more obsessed with my weight and my body. This element is the symptom people are most aware of with anorexia but widely misunderstood. I believe I learned these and picked them up while at the unit with it being the main focus from the staff and the patients. It was the main topic of conversation, how our progress was monitored and what we were defined by in reviews. I was also eating a high calorie meal plan made up of a lot of unhealthy food all week, it is human nature to feel this way, how many times have you said "I feel so fat" after over-eating with an unhealthy takeaway? Though I whole-heartedly believed that I was fat. I constantly asked everybody how I looked, I wanted a detailed explanation every time and I compared myself to every single person I came across, always concluding that I was bigger than all of them.

I did tasks with my key workers at the unit such as drawing around my body to see my outline and at the time it helped me and I realised I was not as big as I thought, but as soon as I walked away I had the thoughts that they lied, did not draw accurately and made it look thin on purpose. "Rex" would always find a reason, I would never know the truth.

I started carrying a blanket around with me everywhere so that I could cover my legs up whenever I sat down – in the car, a restaurant, at home. The sight of my legs would cause the most horrific sensation, stress, and anxiety. If people visited me at home, I wore my dressing gown. Dad took me shopping to buy baggy trousers and over-sized clothes, not party dresses or even a pair of jeans. I could see him looking at what I should be wearing and what he wished he were buying me. He was working in fashion so would have loved a "normal" shopping spree with me, but I could not bear it.

I would envisage cutting my legs to let the fat leak out. I wanted it off me! Get it off me!

"You're a failure. Look at everyone else, you did not go far enough, you are not ill enough."

I was starting to gain weight at the unit, but I had not been following the evening meal plans and had been compulsively exercising. This caused much more confusion in my mind and caused distrust in the unit. Each weekend got worse as I had to eat even less and do even more, sometimes "successfully" dropping nearly 1kg (2.2 lb.) in a weekend.

My mental state was much worse than before the unit. The food plan was excessive and made you gain weight quickly which then caused me to look unnatural and bloated. The therapy was not enough to help me cope.

I was terrified to be at a healthy weight because I was convinced that no-one would care about me anymore. Everyone was interested to talk to me about my illness in the context of if I had gained weight, what I had eaten, what it was like in a unit and never to ask, "how are you *Rachael?*". But maybe there was no Rachael to ask any more. I feared that I would fail at college and it would be known it was because I was stupid and not have the excuse of it being because I was unwell. I feared that I would be vulnerable to bullying again or that I would be lonely. I was beginning to think that I did not want to let go.

My key worker told me she had worked with people on deaths' door who would say they did not go far enough. All I took from this was that I needed to get that ill.

I found out later on that she was right. It is never enough.

"The best anorexic is the one who dies".

New traits were making their way in. I did not have as much control over how much I would eat, so "Rex" gave me new ways. I started eating incredibly slowly and at home, dinner took so long to eat that everyone left the table and I continued for another hour. It was when a meal was finished that I would suffer the mental agony, so I did not want to finish. I was scared to finish.

I was obsessed with the times I could eat; I could not eat dinner at 6:29pm, it *had to be 6:30pm*. I was even more obsessed with calories, I would choose the meal or snack that was 1 calorie less, the relief being immense.

I tied an elastic band around my wrist and repeatedly flicked it to help with the mental pain. Seeing the red lines and bumps appear on my wrist and feeling the physical pain felt so good. The illness was evolving.

I knew nutritional values of most food products. When making light of the situation, my family and friends would quiz me and ask how many calories were in random products in the kitchen. I knew all of them to the exact figure, even the sugar, fat, carbohydrates and salt content.

I was once comfortable with drinking diet soda and this would also fill me up in the day. I then developed a huge fear that it was not really diet and that it was normal soda which was full of sugar and calories. In a pub I would lean over the counter to see them press the right button from the tap, but even when I saw this, I thought that the pipes may be connected wrong and dispense normal soda. I would now only drink diet soda if it was available in the bottle, until I could not trust this either in fear that they had mixed it up in the factory.

In this admission, I was still studying for college and I was allowed to go in for exams. I had called these "starvation days". I was not nervous about the exam and if I would fail. I wanted to succeed at pleasing "Rex".

On the last day of college, I drove past all the students going in dressed up, laughing together and excited for the new stage in life and their future. I was driving to the day unit to eat and panicking about the lunch.

I did go to the college leaving ball, although I was doing an extra year as I had to split my subjects to manage everything.

My sister and my Dad took me shopping for a dress, my Mum could not handle seeing me trying on dresses. They treated me like a normal, excited woman preparing for a big occasion and not someone with an eating disorder, it was amazing. We found a layered dress to hide my ribs and spine and to create more curves, then they accessorised me like a doll. I felt good, not because I saw a skinny frame, nor was I distressed at thinking I was fat. It was possibly the first time in a year that my mood was not dictated by how I felt about my appearance and I was genuinely having fun.

The next day was not so successful and was back to feeling as though I had a big sign over my head labelled "anorexic".

I went to a christening with my other sister, I was so nervous about the buffet, so I did not eat in the morning and then when it came to standing and sitting in the church, I found it too physically exerting and became faint. Despite starving myself to allow for the buffet, I was still too overwhelmed and only managed a small finger sandwich. When "Rex" is in control first thing in the morning, it only tightens its grip through the day. I could not even allow myself a cup of tea in the afternoon. Needless to say that by the evening, I was in a bad way both physically and mentally, I allowed my Dad to make me a diet ready meal because I felt incredibly weak. Even this made "Rex" angry and I asked to play a game with them to "have some fun". I specifically chose a game that involved movement with the real reason being so that I could exercise.

I feel so guilty at the manipulation, using the excuse of family time to please "Rex" and ultimately end up hurting them even more.

I was so lucky with everything I had in life. We were adventurous and outgoing as a family and had so many amazing opportunities given to us.

Tennis is a big part of our family and we went to Wimbledon every year courtesy of a charity my Dad runs called "Tennis For Free".

The year I was stopped from going because of the fear that I would collapse was both difficult and a reality check. My family would not have done this if it was not necessary, so they were serious. But instead of writing how upset I was about missing this day of family tradition and seeing the greats play tennis, I wrote how relieved I was that I would not have to have Pimms, strawberries & cream and to sit still in the matches.

Another great trip was when we surprised my parents by taking them to France for the day. These should be memories I look back on and smile, remembering the adventures and the family time. But all I wrote about was the food, how long I had to sit down for to travel and the mental torment throughout the day.

Another event was my sisters' birthday where we all went to a theme park, I absolutely love days like this with the fun and adrenaline, but all I remember is the pain. My spine, hips and ribs hitting the sides on the rides was incredibly painful, but I could not say anything as I would ruin the day, make it all about me again and I wanted to continue that I was there. I was covered in bruises the following day and worried I had fractured a rib.

I abseiled down the Spinnaker tower with my friend, having to take the day off the unit to do so and got in a lot of trouble. 18 years old and that's how life was. I love adrenaline activities, but at this time I used them to feel something other than the fear from "Rex". I also remember how tiring it was and thought of the calories it was burning and how to get away with refusing the bacon roll that was given when I reached the bottom. I am sure it was fun and an amazing opportunity too…

My whole world was being changed and I was being taken over more and more each day. What used to be genuine enjoyment was now a way to please "Rex".

It was taking everything from me and pushing everyone away. I was watching my best friend, who was once known as "my twin", continue to thrive in life with socialising and parties, planning university and work, enjoying tennis with my sister as her partner now as I was too unwell to continue. Once a potential career, now unable to even play for an hour of fun. It was agonising, but I could not change it. Again I ask, why could I not change it?

Instead of being watched in an exam hall or told off for interrupting a lesson, I was being watched to eat so that I did not throw food away and being told off for eating incorrectly. At one point we were banned from the kitchen due to people swapping lids of build-up shakes (these had our names on for different meal plans, different calories). The kitchen was locked, and we were all watched every minute of the day in the lounge until someone owned up.

I was gaining weight, it was hard not to on this diet, but my head was getting worse, the thoughts stronger. The problem was, people *saw* me as healthier and because I was becoming more obsessed with exercise as a means of control, they thought that I had more energy as well. To start with, I did not want to lose more weight, so I was happy doing nothing on the sofa, but this had evolved into a need to be moving all the time. I could not tell anyone because then I would have to stop, but I was getting less help with people thinking I was doing a lot better. I was screaming out to them, but in my head and just could not let it out loud. I felt like a prisoner to my own mind.

Being at work was not even enough anymore, I had to be doing the most active roles. At the theatre, I had spoken to my boss to be on the coffee shop each shift so that I could eat at the specific time I needed to. I began to use this to be the one to stock up during the show, which involved carrying crates of drinks and snacks up and down stairs. If I was not put on this role and was to sit in the auditorium through the show, I would panic and beg to switch. It was usually fine as the normal people wanted to be paid to sit and watch a good show and did not want the job of stocking up for hours! I was also an outdoors activity instructor at a tree top assault course.

In the morning we were to open the courses which involved going up zip wires, taking down ladders and a lot of physical activity, so I always made sure to open the longest sites as well as the most sites. It became so stressful as everyone was very efficient, so I had to be quick to get there first! At least it made me good at my job and useful for once.

Even when it came to fill the water crates for the course, if someone beat me to it, I would become panicked and anxious. I wanted to be on forest patrol constantly and could not handle being in the cabin or standing on a zip wire platform. It could not be avoided as a part of the job, so I came up with exercises I could do on these roles. It was cold, so it did not look unusual.

We began questioning the day patient system. My parents and friends agreed that the diet was ridiculous. I was in absolute agony and felt so full I thought I was going to be sick but had to keep piling more and more on top. When I tried to speak to the key workers and nurses about it, they would always say, "that's the eating disorder speaking." It was infuriating! You were no longer treated as a person *with* an eating disorder, but just an anorexic inside and out.

When I was struggling so much with how full I was, I asked to have biscuits instead of a milkshake as the thick liquid was just so hard when feeling like that. I was not asking for less, just for help, but I was told if I did not have my milkshake, I may as well not return to the unit.

When my weight was fluctuating with losing over the weekend and gaining in the week, they put me on a "time out" saying I was not engaging in the programme. They had not looked at the fact I was talking in all groups, taking notes, telling nurses what was going on in my mind, no, you are simply a weight chart of numbers and that is all you are. Then if you lost weight on time out, you were discharged. If I was struggling with my weight, as someone diagnosed with anorexia, surely I needed their help more? I was not allowed psychotherapy because I was not at a healthy maintenance weight, but I felt that I needed the help to find the underlying issue in my mind that gave me the *symptom* of being underweight and my fear of gaining weight.

Thankfully my parents were able to come to my reviews at the day unit and they saw how intimidating the staff were. I was not in prison and I had not done anything wrong! I was a victim.

I would not have managed without my parents fighting beside me, continuing to see me as their daughter and as Rachael who needed help right now. It was like being a sane person in an insane place and it was incredibly stressful to try and prove I was still an intellectual being. It took me back to the days of being bullied when no-one would believe me except for my parents.

I somehow gained weight on my week out of the unit and they also somehow convinced me to continue the day patients programme.

From the first day back, it was a regretful decision.

I was messaging my friends, the only contact I had with them at that moment, and the staff shouted at me for using external sources for help and not them. I spoke to the key workers every day, mostly to say I was so confused and did not understand my own mind, and the last response I had was, "well what do you want us to do? Pry it out of you?"

It is a part of my personality to want everyone to be happy and for everyone to like me, if someone is upset or even seems unhappy then I will believe it is my fault. This was heightened with suffering from anorexia and is still something I struggle with today. However, I do not think that this was purely paranoia that led me to feel this way at the unit.

The staff did not engage with me, would not smile at me in passing and did not talk to me outside timetabled sessions when they were obliged to.

I had lost 100g in my first week back on the unit after "time out" and I was called into an unplanned meeting. This meant my parents were not present. I can remember how intimidated I felt, how scared I was in a room full of people telling me they were not happy with me. That is all they called me in for, not to change my treatment plan, just to exert their authority and power. With this, "Rex" made the team become my enemy too. I can see why.

The following week I lost weight again. I was in so much fear of what the staff would do and what they would say. I did not feel comforted or able to talk about it, they would not want to help me as to why, they would just look at the crime I had committed. I had my planned key work session that day and was just told the same thing as every week for half an hour.

"It will get stronger as you lose weight." - then help me stop this. "It will kill you." - I am not choosing to die.

"What caused it?" - That is why I am here, for you to help me find out.

"You have to eat." - Genius.

The friend I had made in the unit, the true friend I previously spoke about, got discharged because she was not making progress. She was told she had to maintain for a few months as an outpatient to be allowed to come back and she admitted she knew she would lose weight. Their response was not to be hard on herself as it is rare for someone to recover first time and not end up in hospital.

I still had my parents, and we would not give up. My Mum asked if I would see a hypnotherapist, I would try anything. I found a glimmer of hope with her, she helped me understand the subconscious a lot more and gave analogies to rationalise what was happening in my mind. Though this helped with the confusion and lowered my stress levels, I was unable to be "fully" hypnotised as I would not let go and I would not let someone else have the control, or "Rex" would not. I still use a technique she taught me to calm the nervous system down, which is called "7-11 breathing", inhaling slowly for 7 seconds and exhaling for 11 seconds.

She also said she could tell when "Rachael" was walking into the room and when "Rex" was. I admit I am a slight sceptic with these therapies, and I would usually think this was something that was always said, however, my friends and family had described the same differences in my posture, body language and my eyes. I was completely unaware of it and that was a scary and unnerving sensation.

This was the first of many forms of therapy that I tried which were funded by my parents and for that I am incredibly grateful, but also feel guilty that it did not cure me.

The team at the Day Hospital were not happy when they found I was seeking external help, telling me it was conflicting and would not work with the programme. That raised many questions in my mind.

When I did gain 800g in one week, I panicked. I had been exercising a lot and restricting food in the evenings and on the weekend. When I spoke to my key worker for reassurance, she said she did not know why it increased so much, but we did not need to know. It was not the most reassuring response and made my belief that they did not know what they were doing even stronger, my trust in them reducing further. Why was it not the same relaxed and unknown reason when I lost a mere 100g? When that happened, I was in trouble and it was my fault.

I don't know how I kept so motivated throughout this, the writing helped and I kept self-rationalising what "Rex" would say to me, using all my strength to do so.

"I am lucky food is my medicine. Those with cancer go through chemotherapy with many horrible side effects."

"If I survive and live a long life, do I want to look back on these years and remember food and weight? As opposed to that fun night when…, that moment we laughed so much…"

"Everyone dies but not everyone lives."

"Why do I want to belong in the unit and be unmotivated, unenthusiastic and with no passion or dreams?"

When I had these moments of motivation and positivity, some others in the unit would turn on me and say it was not real, there is no miracle moment, it would not last… It is unsurprising that people had turned bitter in the unit and I do not blame them if they had endured this programme several times, I admire them more than anything. However, it did not create a good environment for recovery.

I do not know why or how I stayed in the unit. I think I knew that it would be a lot worse if I had nowhere to go and that it gave me permission to eat for at least half of my week.

I was about to find out as I was granted a week off to go on holiday with my family and a friend. I was told that if I lost weight I would be discharged.

It did not start off well. I was thrown by the early morning flight and did not know when I was allowed to eat because all the timings were different. When it came to choosing something at the airport for the flight my sister said, "sorry, but I am going to push you this holiday." I had to do the 7-11 breathing technique to prevent the panic and I wanted to run back home, do not make me go on holiday!

At the hotel, the first thing I noticed was that the bowls and plates were different. How would I know how much cereal to have? Everyone else admired the scenery and the beauty of where we were while I went to a shop and get portioned yoghurt pots so that I could cope.

At every meal I was comparing with my family and friend, who did not have the biggest appetites, and so I found it incredibly hard and became angry and stressed at them all. Not what you want on a holiday. Again, I apologise to all of you.

One night we were given ice cream at the end of the meal by the restaurant. Everyone laughed at my face dropping in fear! But this made the situation easier, and I managed to eat the one scoop of ice cream.

To begin with I managed to let go a little bit, be my old, or real, self and enjoy the holiday. I had forgotten what it was like and these glimmers meant so much to us all.

I wore a bikini without worrying I looked fat, in fact, my body image was a lot better on holiday. I ate ice creams, had cocktails, I ate meals at different times, I laughed, I had the energy to have fun. I did not do any hidden exercise, I swam a little and did the normal sight-seeing. My sister said I surprised her and did really well. That boosted my morale so much, making me wonder if I am better off out of the unit?

But gradually "Rex" became more prominent, triggered by a night when we had a barbecue on the beach before stargazing. What an incredible opportunity! All I remember was the bread, fatty meat and cheese for dinner. The fear energised "Rex" who ruined the whole evening.

My friend was really upset with me most of the time from then on and told me she was having nightmares each night about me dying, like my Mum did. My family were used to living with me whereas it was a shock for my friend to see the reality when with me 24/7. I was also becoming angry at my Mum and my friend who were not eating much. "Rex" was using this to make me eat less, show me I was eating way too much and worst of all, to ruin my relationship with them and start attacking my army. This had already started happening at home with my Mum and caused strain on our relationship throughout my illness. "Rex" attacked her with full force but thankfully, she knew it was not me and that I was unwell.

The day before returning to the unit, I had a huge surge of positivity. I bought jeans to wear instead of the baggy clothes, when I had to wear jeans that were UK size 6, I was shocked, thinking I was at least a UK size 10. I did not want to play tennis because it was exercise, I went to an independent café with my friend so that I did not know the calories and chatted for hours about everything but the eating disorder, she begged me not to go back to "Rex" and to stay this way.

I woke up early on the day I was to return to the unit with such anxiety about being weighed and what the outcome would be.

I had lost half a kilo. A discharge date was set with a "four-week phase out", where you gradually reduce the days at the unit and given more independence when there.

Considering I clearly was not free from "Rex", this seemed pointless and again to just do it correctly by the books for their paperwork.

On the final days I became quite fearful as I realised how much I had come to rely on the unit, knowing I would be allowed to eat when I was there, feeling a little more protected from "Rex" with a form of help down the corridor should I need it. When I leave, if "Rex" wanted to attack, nothing would be there to stop it.

As I slowly returned to college and to the real world, I started to become more depressed. I was back in the position where I knew I could not get better without the help and I knew "Rex" would continue to be strong in my mind, so I had two possible outcomes. I would either maintain at this stage, where I could exist in a life but not live a life, or I would get worse. But now that I would not be allowed on the day patient programme, would I be left until I became "ill enough" to be eligible for more intensive treatment?

I truly and honestly did not want either of these options, I just wanted to be well and to be free.

3

The First Relapse

"Things are tough. I've been out of hospital for six weeks and feel as though I'm on the edge of a cliff trying to decide whether to jump or continue the huge, exhausting climb ahead."

I went to Ireland with my friend who was still right there beside me, since the beginning. Initially I did really well but for some reason on the last day my mood plummeted and I was in sudden fear of everything as though I was going to be punished for having a good time away and neglecting to please "Rex".

A week later, my mood had not picked up, I was becoming clinically depressed. I was trying to cling on to the motivation I still had inside me, but it was rapidly fading.

I wanted to be back in Farnham Hospital, at least with people who were in the battle with me and people to stop "Rex" taking full control, even if it was done in the wrong way. I was trying to keep on top of college as well, it was all too much.

My Dad hugged me and just said, "What can I do, I just want to click my fingers and have my Rachy back."

Then came a night I will never forget.

I had been in London for the day with my sister. I had every intention to make her proud, do really well and have a nice day out, but that did not happen.

I put on a brave face from the torture that was going on in my mind and was up to my antics of managing to get away with not eating much and to walk, and walk, and walk. I cannot remember anything else about the day, until the agonising pain I was in when we got on the train home. It was a pain I had experienced before but not to this level and I know it is when my body is in starvation mode. Sharp stabbing pain through my ribs, in my stomach and my kidneys. I curled up on the seat on the train and went straight to bed when I got home. Only I could not sleep from the pain. At 2am, I went dizzy and light-headed and started shaking. Again, I had experienced this before, but again, not to this extent. I literally crawled down the stairs and got 1 mini piece of cereal out the box, it was all I could manage to try and help myself. I could not manage to do any more.

I went into my parents' room, I said that I do not feel so good, got into their bed and curled up in between them. They said they felt me flop onto them and they knew. They knew my body was giving up, and so did I. The pain was excruciating and was rapidly taking any strength that I did have left. I was very weak, but my head was strong, so when Dad asked if he could get me a cup of tea with sugar to help me through, it was too much and I could not. My parents were so distressed but tried to stay strong as they just held me tight, allowing me to be at peace and die in their arms. This takes an amazing bond to do, an amazing sense of understanding and incredibly strong parents. But I did wake up in the morning. To live another day of torture. I am not entirely sure that I was glad I woke up, but someone was looking over me and it was not my time to go yet.

I was still in agonising pain and when I went to the toilet, my urine was black and foaming. My kidneys giving up.

Thank goodness my parents gave me strength, thank goodness they are the most heroic parents you would ever imagine, as I pulled myself back from this night with determination. It was not too late; I had survived, and I was meant to live.

I called my friend who was still right there beside me since the beginning, she took me out for coffee and I decided to have a muffin as well. At this time that was a huge step and I said I would have half of it but then went for the whole thing. I felt elated with a sense of liberation to fight back at "Rex" and not let it take my life. After speaking about body image, she took me to Hollister to try on some jeans, I asked if they had a smaller size as they were too big and was told they were the smallest, size 00. I felt embarrassed, I was pleased I felt ashamed and shocked as opposed to happy.

This lasted a few weeks and we were becoming hopeful again. Why could that not last? It began to decline, my meal plan slowly reducing and I became sad and angry again.

Mum was very emotionally affected as I fluctuated and our relationship became more strained. She did not have the biggest appetite and with the worry for me, her own eating had been affected which only made me, or "Rex", angry. She was telling me I needed to eat but was not herself. I know she was healthy and not at risk of dying but "Rex" did not care, it wanted to use this to attack her.

I was in a position where deep down I wanted to go to hospital to get full support, however I could not tell anyone this or ask as then it would be "my choice" and was not allowed. So I wanted something to happen to me physically, something to go wrong where I had to be taken to hospital without a choice. Quite often I would have the desire to jump off the roof of my house so that I would break a bone and be taken to hospital. It would be less painful than defying "Rex". The song "I can't live, with or without you" played at this point which was exactly how I felt with "Rex" now.

It was around Christmas and I was working at the theatre for the pantomime. This was hard work and we would watch an average of twenty shows in three weeks! The stewards would pull together as a team and have fun through it and went for meals and drinks after shifts. I joined in when they went to a restaurant I found "safe" for me to eat at. That night I woke up having a big panic attack wondering if they give me the wrong meal. It was 3am and I was searching for the pictures, desperately trying to remember what my meal looked like to match with their menu and work out what I had.

I had been out of the day patient unit for two months and had a doctor's appointment to monitor how I was doing. I had lost 1.5kg (3.3lb) with my weight now down to 37kg (81.5lb). 5kg (11lb) less than when I first went to the doctor and now with a BMI of fourteen. Things were getting worse and the doctor was angry, she rang the day unit where the manager said she was not concerned.

How low does your weight have to be to be of concern? My BMI was low, but my mood was lower, and my head had strong demons in it, why would they not help me?

"Rex" convinced me that I was wearing lighter clothes than before and I had drunk less and that is why my weight had dropped so I still did not need the help.

That is two against one so I must not need help, I must be ok.

Christmas Day came back around. Remembering saying the previous year that the next Christmas I will be able to join in with everything! Or not. Even worse.

The mince pie that caused such distress the last year was not even discussed as there was not a glimmer of hope I would have one. I had my own dinner entirely. Even the two cheese and crackers with light soft cheese was weighed and in a meal plan made with my therapist. When I nibbled a roasted chestnut and put a marshmallow on my diet hot chocolate, I was tormented by my head and my day was completely ruined.

It is torture to have such a desire to just feast like everyone else, they are all happy while I am miserable, it is such a simple answer! All I could do was watch the life I wanted but what seemed impossible for me to have. I hoped that next Christmas I would be going to bed stuffed full of food and happiness.

My friends' birthday came around. Last year I joined in with little energy and calculating the drinks I had, but pushed myself for her as it was the least I could do after all she had done for me.

This year I was not even allowed to attempt it. My Dad walked me down the road to her house to wish her a Happy Birthday. I sat and watched them all dress up in beautiful outfits, doing their hair and make-up, pre-drinking, and dancing with so much joy before Dad collected me an hour later to go home for my hot chocolate and bed. I was incredibly distressed, and my mind was telling me what a loser I was. Though the reason I was not joining in was because of the demon in my head, it did not let me see that, I could not see that, and it was an attack on myself as a person. A loser and a failure.

My motivation and determination somehow shone through after this instead of plummeting and I wrote a letter to Mum and Dad telling them to push and challenge me, or "Rex", from now on. I had to jump on these moments and have them in a permanent form as it could go just as quickly as it came. I had written everything I hate about the illness; losing all my friends, feeling ashamed to continue talking about it, tearing my family apart, unable to concentrate on studying. So why could I not let go?

I was trying so hard and I was truly fighting the whole way through.

An analogy I used for this stage was: *"I'm stuck on a mountain. I am in a secure place for now and have enough supplies to scrape through the days for a while. I can wait here in the hope rescue will come, or there is a ledge a few steps away that I could jump off and hope to land somewhere in reach of being rescued, I would just be a little more battered and bruised… but it could be fatal. I cannot continue climbing, I might get a little higher but there is no way I will reach the top without specialist equipment. The best option seems to be sliding down to make a rescue more likely."*

At my next doctor's appointment, my weight had maintained at 37kg (81.5lb) and I was therefore classified as "stable" and sent on my way.

My parents gave me an option of a lifeline, to go to a private clinic in Norwich for intensive inpatient treatment. However, because this would be privately and by choice, they would have to pay for it. I would only be able to stay for six weeks at £ 2,500 per week. The guilt this would cause was too much when I was told I was not ill enough by doctors and considered it a self-inflicted illness. But my mood was at rock bottom, I was existing and not living and barely existing at that. All I longed for was to be able to sit in the cinema and have popcorn, to be able to stay at a friend's house for dinner, or to allow a cup of tea to be made for me.

That evening I became my own worst enemy. I had over-heard my family talking to each other about how much I play them off each other and how horrible I can be towards them. It was true. "Rex" used this conversation, a lot.

I decided I could not accept help, I did not deserve it because I was such an awful human being. I deserved to suffer and that was the reason I had anorexia, to hide away the truly horrible person I was. I would not talk to anyone about it anymore and I would not seek any form of help, let alone have my parents pay for treatment.

I was in self-destruct mode, my mood and my self-hatred had spiralled downhill, everyone noticing and everyone affected by it.

One day at work when I was having a difficult day in my mind, I did not manage to eat very much, and when I got home Dad had cooked the dinner that I had planned to have, only he had drowned the potatoes and vegetables in oil. His face lit up when I walked in as he felt proud to surprise me with dinner when I came home, knowing I had chosen it so felt safe to do this for me.

Oil was a huge fear of mine so that bomb in the minefield was set off again. I can still remember the heart breaking look on my Dad's face and how it dropped and when he said in the most defeated voice, "I got it wrong again."

He did not even give up at that point and drained the oil off which resulted in burnt food and did not relieve my panic as the food had absorbed oil. Real Rachael is a people-pleaser and a daddy's girl, so

I managed to pull it together, get some strength and said I would have it. He put one too many potatoes on my plate which caused me to freak out at him again. All he could do was sigh and take it off. I took an hour to eat it in misery and silence, took sleeping tablets and went to bed.

Finishing this entry off again with, *"I AM SUCH A HORRIBLE PERSON."* And *"I am so sorry, my poor Daddy."*

When I did manage to speak to my Dad about what I had overheard, he helped me to see that it is not just me suffering and that accepting treatment would be for all of us. I was making everyone's life difficult and a living nightmare.

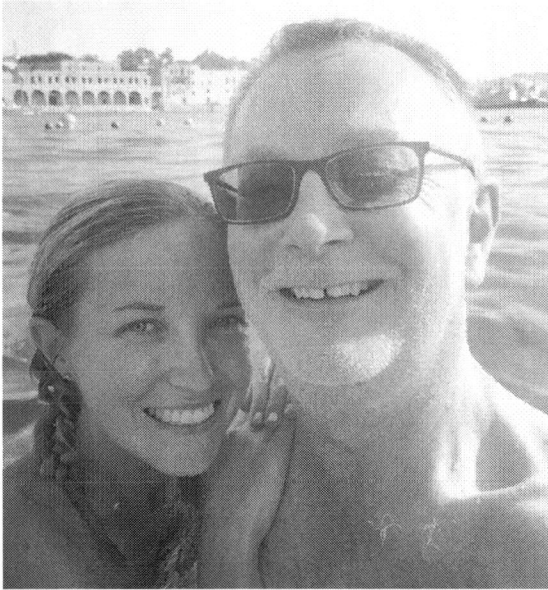

4

The First Inpatient Admission

In February 2012, I arrived at the private clinic which was four hours away from home. Though it felt like a family home in the way it was set up and not within a hospital, so it was a friendly and safe environment to begin recovery in.

Upon arrival, I was taken straight upstairs to have my suitcase checked and things that could be used for harm confiscated such as razors, scissors, tweezers.

I was then taken to a small, very warm room as I had to strip to my underwear to be weighed by two members of staff which felt so intimidating at first, but soon became a part of daily life. At this clinic, we went on the scales backwards so that we did not know what our weight was with this potentially causing a lot of trauma.

When the assessment was finished, I went to say goodbye to my Mum and Dad, I would have minimal contact with them during the admission to focus on recovery. Normally parents are emotional at waving their children off to go travelling or to university, but we had an incredibly emotional goodbye with so much fear, but also hope that this would save me.

From my first day the feeling of guilt began. Why was I there? My parents were spending all their money on something unnecessary as I looked around to see so many incredibly unwell patients, both physically and in their behaviours towards food. I was not that bad, nowhere near.

I was told that I would not be allowed upstairs once I came down in the morning until going back to bed at night, I should bring everything I would need down to the lounge and if I needed anything else, I would have to find a support worker to get it for me. It felt over the top and again unnecessary for me.

I began on the half portions and I found that I was still hungry. It was a lot more than I was eating at home but now I was being given permission I realised how hungry my body was. I can see that clearly now, however at the time, I thought of myself as a fraud for being hungry and this was more ammunition for "Rex" to make me believe that I did not need to be there.

A big goal of mine was to be able to have a cup of tea or coffee whenever I wanted it and how I like it, which was simply with a little milk and half a teaspoon of sugar. It was a challenge of mine throughout my illness, and I think it was also linked with it being a little life pleasure which I did not deserve, as well as the extra calories. I asked for a cup of tea with my afternoon snack, feeling safe to do so with having the support there. But my head screamed at me for the rest of the day for being greedy.

For the first three nights I was woken at 2am to have my blood sugar checked. The support worker tip-toed in with a torch for you to put your arm out for the finger-prick test and if the glucose levels were below four you had to have two biscuits. I did not sleep well as I was panicking about this and watching the time, biscuits in the middle of the night would be horrendous.

One of the nights my test was 3.9. *"Nooooooo!"*. However, they decided that it was unfair to put me through that torment when it was 0.1 below and said they would check on me in another hour, when it was back to level four. Phew! That is how this clinic was, caring and considerate. They wanted to help.

I became good friends with another patient who was in a similar position to me. He was outgoing and bubbly and got me through that admission without a doubt. I have many memories, such as sitting on the floor just rolling a ball to each other for an hour and chatting, the first time I had allowed myself to sit down for so long by choice. Then there was the time he came back from an evening out incredibly drunk! He decided he was a cat and made everyone laugh so much, the sound of laughter was so freeing and liberating.

We stayed in contact for a short while after the admission until one day I heard nothing, I do not know what happened to him to this day and never could find out.

But if I thought being in the day hospital was bad, being an inpatient was a whole new level. Living with nine other patients with anorexia was intense, the constant comparisons with each other, the competitiveness of who had been and who was the most ill. From the conversation, some patients clearly did not want to get better and would try to give tips on how to beat the system in treatment, it took incredible strength to ignore this as I could not simply walk away, I was confined to one house and in one room.

The day hospital diet included a lot of food, but I did not ever eat properly when I went back home and now I was having to eat a full meal plan all day, I can never explain just how full I was! At this clinic, there was a chef preparing fresh food and I got on well with her as I appreciated the taste of the meals and would complement them – it must be such a hard job to cook for people who do not want it, hate it, and sometimes throw it!

We chose our meals each day. The support staff would come round in the evening to ask what we wanted for breakfast, then after breakfast would ask for lunch and dinner out of two options. This would take a very long time with staff trying to help us make such a difficult choice. Though it almost became something to do in the day.

The full diet consisted of a breakfast with cereal, toast, fruit and juice followed by a mid-morning snack. We then had a main meal for lunch with fruit as dessert, followed by an afternoon snack. In the evening we had another main meal followed by a snack before bed.

The meals were large portions and the snacks were in the form of a "snack basket" where we would go into the kitchen to a selection of snacks chosen by the staff and have to choose what to have. It was quite an event! People were desperately trying to look at the nutrition values but being stopped by staff and refusing to be first to choose to be able to see what everyone else had. I had a war in my head about choosing what to have based on what I had eaten earlier or had later as I felt a compulsive need to have a balance to such an extent it was nearly impossible. I could not have an oat bar is I had porridge in the morning, I could not have potato chips if I had potatoes with dinner, I could not have sugar if the fruit for dessert was of a high sugar content, and so on. It would have been easier if like most of the other patients I simply wanted the lowest calorie option.

It was a high calorie diet and filling, especially when I was not allowed to move all day and was just sitting on the sofa.

We had therapy groups in either the same room we were in all day or the room opposite which was a welcome change of scenery. These groups were much more beneficial than in the day hospital and we also had art groups and the option to have piano lessons.

The staff were around us all day and played games with us, had normal chats, laughed and watched movies. They were fantastic and I have fond memories of all of them.

I began to be able to relax and watch Netflix on my laptop, this became an hour of allowance to not think or feel guilty, it was blissful. The slight tune that comes before any Netflix show still takes me right back to the exact sofa that I was curled up on or the bed I was in with my headphones on and spikes an instant reaction of emotion in me. It was a huge step and a great relief to have an hour of respite within the torment.

Halfway through my admission I was able to go out with a staff member to tackle challenges such as snacks out, clothes shopping and treating myself. I remember a time when I mentioned I could not buy blusher because it would make me look healthy and I did not want to spend money on myself. She challenged me and supported me in getting it and when I did, I was stressed about it for over a week and it took a lot more support to start wearing it.

I was making a lot of progress and was beginning to find my mind manageable. My parents came to visit one month later, and I was incredibly nervous as to how they would think I looked. I needed staff support to get changed out of my pyjamas and to decide what to wear. When I answered the door, I clutched my pillow until my Mum shrieked and jumped at me to give me a hug – I have tears in my eyes at this amazing memory. They were here to see ME, their daughter, not to analyse my body.

We went into the city and to a café which we will all remember very well! A quirky tea-room that was NOT a chain restaurant for the first time in years. We shared a selection of sandwiches and I was anticipating the panic and anxiety, but it never came.

I needed a snack in the afternoon, I could have lied about this, but I told them I needed it. My Mum could see how anxious I was when I went to get my latte, so when I turned around she gave me a loving look and mouthed the words, "you can do it".

I was even allowed to play tennis with them. I was nervous about this as exercise used to feed "Rex" and I would find it hard to stop and want to move more and more. But when we played, I just had fun and enjoyed it, genuinely enjoyed it.

To finish off the day, we went to a Thai restaurant on a boat where I had a carefree glass of wine with my meal, and we were all sat relaxed with genuine smiles.

The happiness of that day is indescribable.

I had come such a long way in a short time that in my meeting with the team and my parents, we decided I would stay an extra week to consolidate everything, to give myself a really good chance of continuing to a full recovery. My parents had to fund this as well and I actually asked them to allow me this extra week. It was another big step for me to ask for this chance, but I had so much hope this time and did not ever want to be taken back to "Rex".

That last week turned out to be very difficult. "Rex" was angry I was still there and was getting ready to attack. I was eating meals incredibly slowly; I do not know why and I could not make myself eat normally no matter how much I tried.

I went for my last lunch out with the support worker and I had a sparkling drink with my lunch. When I realised that she had read the label wrong and had read per 100ml and not per can, I completely freaked out. She had to calm me down and talk me through it, to look around at how many people were drinking it without fear and if I enjoyed it, which I did, then why did I have to panic?

Why were things suddenly so hard again? It made me concerned leaving the following week, very concerned.

The other patients were complimenting me on being an inspiration to them, that I had been so determined and strong.

However, I can see now that I had been hiding many emotions and showing these would have been stronger. Allowing myself to have the tantrums when I was in turmoil or screaming the house down when I was screaming inside would have been stronger.

Discharge day came with an extreme range of mixed emotions. I went into the garden with the staff, the other patients and my parents. We all had a pink balloon and everyone stood together saying something positive about me. I found it hard to receive compliments, I still struggle with this today, but I just held my parents tight who were in floods of tears. At the end, everyone was in tears and we let the balloons go, watching them float away until we could no longer see them, and it was time for me to go home. It was the first time there was a send-off like this at the clinic.

When I left the door and got into the car, I started crying uncontrollably. You make close connections with everyone, I had lived with them for 7 weeks and shared so much, been on an emotional rollercoaster with them and it was a very caring and special place. But I was also scared. I wanted to stay, "Rex" was ready for me, I know it was.

After I was discharged, I stopped writing for a while and started living. I felt confident going out with friends in my new clothes and having fun again. I went for days out with friends and family, to restaurants, people's houses for dinner, joined in on a girls night where I allowed them to make me drinks and we danced and laughed all night long!

A friend I have known since we were babies came to stay for a week and we went on a shopping spree where I bought nice clothes such as jeans and dresses as opposed to baggy clothes or pyjamas! We went to Wimbledon together and being allowed to go again that year meant a lot to me.

I played in the tennis tournament at our local club, having missed out for a few years, and I actually won! It was like I had my entire past, or normal, life back.

But it was by no means a miraculous recovery and I still had to fight the demons to stop them from taking over.

When I played in another tennis tournament and played badly, I became so defeated and took it out on my food with refusing to eat a proper lunch or a snack. My head told me I was undeserving of it. These situations had occurred a few times but would not last and I would start worrying about slipping back into the awful illness and put a stop to it.

I had appointments with the medical team every week to check my weight and blood pressure.

When I was first weighed after discharge and saw it was 46.5kg (102.5lb), to my surprise I was happy and not panicked! I gained 7kg (15.5lb) in 7 weeks and managed to maintain it as an outpatient. I was seeing another private therapist but began to book to see her as I needed her, as opposed to on a weekly basis, things were going very well.

It came to exam week at college and I had been studying to the best of my abilities while in hospital. I was incredibly stressed and constantly going over notes with my parents each evening, I think they knew the context better than I did by the end!

I sat my Psychology exam, ironically this is when I had a strange experience of my own mind. I could not concentrate on the questions and I kept reading them over and over but not grasping any of the words. I had to try and write something and when I had written two pages, I realised I had answered the wrong question entirely as the words seemed to click in my brain. I became so stressed that I had to leave the room where I began crying hysterically and could not catch my breath until my tutor found me and calmed me down. She said that I should not be hard on myself, that I had been through a lot and perhaps should not complete the exam. I had worked too hard to take that option so went back in and did the best I could to complete it. I went to play tennis with my Dad after the exam and had forgotten how to hold my tennis racket! Dad found this quite amusing at first until he saw just how distressed I was becoming and was not exaggerating or joking that I could not remember. I started crying in fear and frustration so we had to go home.

That evening I had a tennis match with my Mum and still could not remember. I ran off crying yet again, trying to stop another panic attack. When I managed to find my strength to return, my friend and my mum had to keep positioning my hand correctly and I gripped on as tight as I could so that I did not let go and forget again. Never giving up on anything!

I went on holiday with my parents and Sophie, the friend I have known all my life and is there no matter how far apart or for how long. It was the first holiday since we went to Greece where things did not end well, nor did the holiday before that.

We were going to Egypt and it did not start well at the airport with the flight being three hours delayed and therefore the plan we had being altered, which I still found difficult. Instead of eating a planned sandwich on the plane, I was now to eat at a restaurant. The healthy meal I chose was out of stock and so I chose plain chicken with brown rice, we were concerned.

On the plane we got another meal, I had managed to pull myself back from the episode at the airport and enjoy this as well as the surprise bottle of champagne that my Dad ordered us on the aeroplane.

Upon arrival I got a cocktail and was feeling nothing but happiness, thank goodness!

The rest of the time I was better than I had ever been with enjoying all types of food at the hotel, restaurants, barbecues on a boat and in a desert. The best thing was not having to muster all of my strength to do this and somehow managing with ease. Even when I became horrifically sick with food poisoning, I was desperate to get better as opposed to my mind thinking of it as a way to lose weight.

Typically this occurred when we were going on quad bikes and camels through the desert. Most people would have not been able to go, but I had learnt to push through pain and I did not want to be a cause of problems again with illness or let people down. When it got incredibly bad, one of the guides went off on his quad bike through the desert and brought back camels' milk which is supposed to help the stomach. This would have completely freaked me out before, but I did not think twice about trying it… and it did work!

I could have used being unwell as an excuse to not eat in the evening, but I continued to enjoy a barbecue full of "fatty and scary" meats and dishes in the evening.

I wore a bikini each day with confidence and did not hide away from compliments. Again, it was not that the thoughts about my body had gone, the feelings attached were not as strong and I was able to push them aside.

I could relax, sunbathe, read my book on the balcony and not feel guilty about it but just enjoy it as most people do.

My friend and I went to the beach parties to dance through the night, making up for all the events I had missed out on.

It was the happiest I had been since I could remember and showed how life in recovery could be. I was not being complacent; I was not free from anorexia and still had the destructive thoughts, but I could rationalise them and not be consumed by them. Also, they were only my own thoughts and no longer another voice.

I had missed out on a lot at an important and fun stage of life. Now that I was doing well and had worked so hard, I wanted to experience life and therefore decided to volunteer in Ghana for a month and apply to work in France for the summer afterwards. It kept me motivated to stay well to experience life outside of hospitals.

Why would I ever go back to a life of isolation, despair and being controlled?

5

Volunteering in Ghana

I was not recovered by any means and some may say I was trying to run away from it all. I would say that deep down I knew I was going to be victim to "Rex" again either way and while I was well enough, I wanted to have achieved something in my life, to experience something other than hospitals and to help others instead of them helping me.

So I went to volunteer in Ghana for four weeks, a break for everyone!

When I waved goodbye to my parents at the airport, I got such a rush of adrenaline and a sense of freedom! I was now completely responsible for my own health, money, and time. I was actually looking forward to the 7-hour flight with forced relaxation to watch movies, eat and drink… I was certainly much better than I once was!

When we landed, it was a three-hour journey from the airport to the volunteer house, but we had entertainment along the way! Within 10-minutes, we were at traffic lights and the driver was buying water from baskets which were being balanced on ladies' heads. A little further on the road seemed to stop and we were suddenly driving over a bumpy desert avoiding potholes and piles of sand, while everyone flashed their lights and beeped their horns… we had no idea what was going on and just looked at each other in hope! The driver had put English music on for us quite loudly, possibly to distract us, and I just sat eating chocolate, smiling, and loving life.

Suddenly the driver stopped and we had police surrounding the car holding big guns, I was not so relaxed anymore! We were asked to get out of the car while they searched it and spoke to the driver, everyone seeming very calm. We simply got back in the car and carried on. When we asked the driver what was going on, he did not realise we would be slightly scared by the situation as it is routine in Ghana and would happen along every journey. He was right and through our stay in Ghana, we did get used to it!

We arrived at the house at 1am so we crept in quietly to not wake anyone, only to walk in on a big party! I was exhausted and everything was already so surreal that my head could not comprehend what was going on, so we just went with it and joined in as if we had just returned home to friends we had known for years. Going to bed at 4am, we woke up at 7am to begin our first day in Ghana.

We did not go to the school for volunteering that day as the staff showed us around and how to live our new lives for the next month. The first thing was the shower. We had to fill a small bucket with cold water at the worlds slowest tap in the kitchen, taking about twenty minutes. You then took it to the bathroom and used an even smaller pot to scoop the water and pour it over yourself. If there was a storm, even in the middle of the night, we would all run outside with our shampoo to have a decent wash in a power shower!

Sometimes the water ran out from the storage outside so we washed using baby wipes, after a sweaty day of work in 40C heat, it took a lot of baby wipes and we would pray for a big storm to arrive! We also had to fill a bucket of water to flush the toilet, so we had a rule that we did not do this if you only went for a wee to save water! Life in Africa!

The staff of the volunteer house made us our first breakfast, which was an omelette and flatbread. Little did we know that would be the best meal we would have for quite some time!

The owners of the volunteering company came to meet us and took us into the town to get our SIM cards and change money. There was a man sitting at a fold out table with pen, paper and a wallet to give us both the SIM cards and change of money!

The next task was to go to the supermarket, well, a backroom with a few shelves of random products. We got powdered milk, cornflakes and packet noodles. To begin with it was so hot that we did not have the biggest appetites, (ironically an anorexics dream), but later on I jumped at any opportunity to eat a good meal whenever we could!

When everyone returned from working, we played a makeshift version of table tennis and then went to the local bar. The volunteers were very well known there as we were the only customers! I discovered that you could not get any diet drinks and only Alco pops, cider or vodka with full sugar soda. I became very anxious about this initially but then laughed at feeling like I was at a house party as a sixteen-year-old, something I missed out on and could now experience.

As it had cooled down and after a few drinks I realised how hungry I was, so we were pointed in the direction of "chicken and rice lady". It was an interesting meal, the rice tasted nice, but the chicken was greasy skin on a bone, the chickens did not have meat on them here. We were sat on the side of the road in the dark and told we were best not to be able to see what we were eating. I did initially panic at the grease and not knowing what it was but again refused to let "Rex" in, this was my time.

Waking up the next day at 7am, we were going to the school to start our first day of volunteering. Kwasi came to pick us up in the minibus each day and we all were tightly packed in for the forty-five-minute journey. On the way we stopped in a town where we could get some breakfast from the shop or from a stand with a lady who made the biggest omelette sandwich with a whole loaf of bread or doughnut balls. This would be our only meal until the evening before a long and active day.

When we arrived at the school, a little girl ran straight over to me and gave me a hug. I picked her up and spun her around, the smile and laughter was amazing. Then the rest of the children came over and it was quite overwhelming. Hundreds of children running over and shouting, "hello ma'am", "What is your name?", "Do you have a pencil", "Will you be my teacher?"

The school was in an open area in the middle of the village that the children lived in. It was one long, wooden shack split into four classrooms with handmade wooden benches inside and a chalkboard at the front. I began teaching the youngest group and I taught them songs such as "head, shoulders, knees and toes", "Old McDonald had a farm" and "Simon says" which caused a lot of laughter! We then did basic maths and pronouncing of each other's names. I have never seen such an attentive group of young children who were so desperate to learn, if we did not start teaching right away, all the children would constantly be asking and pulling us into the classrooms. They were all so appreciative of being given a pencil and piece of paper, in fact we had to control the class when giving them out as we were bombarded when we brought these luxury items with us.

At lunchtime thousands of nuts were delivered with piles put in front of each child to crack open one at a time and were not allowed to continue learning until they did so. These would be sold for a profit to the "head teacher." It was incredibly tough to watch and we wanted to help them so much, but we were not as skilled and if too many were broken, they would be caned. That would have been harder to watch and feeling to blame.

We could not just stand feeling helpless, so we went to paint the I.C.T lab which had been built and donated recently by other volunteers. The children were soon going to see and use computers for the first time.

On the way back to the house on the minibus I got emotional with it being a hard hitting and overwhelming day. We were there to help for 4 weeks; this was their daily life.

The next day at the school was manic as two volunteers were leaving, so they had brought gifts with them of water, biscuits and whistle toys. This brought more joy than you could imagine, more than when children are given the latest technology, mobile phones and money in our first world society. However, we were about to introduce them to the world of technology and took a few children to see the computers that had been put into the I.C.T room. They stood in stunned silence with a look of awe on their faces, and we had not even shown them how they worked yet. The funniest thing was when we turned them on, the part they loved the most was standing by the fan at the back of the monitor as it kept them cool for once!

When returning back from the I.C.T lab, I experienced something I will never forget. I came across an extremely ill child on the side of a road from malnourishment. He was on his own and when I found the head teacher to let him know, he waved his hand as if it did not matter and the child was of no use anymore.

I asked about his family and he just shook his head, so I sat down and put my arm around him. He looked up at me in disbelief and surprise at being cared for and I remember those yellow eyes making contact with mine.

I sang nursery rhymes to him and tried to give him some water which he threw up immediately.

The team that ran the volunteering groups found us and they took over. I never knew what happened from there, though I can take a good guess.

I felt so guilty that I had been going down a route that was making me that ill and malnourished but with food on offer, when he would have given anything to have had the chance to eat.

The staff and other volunteers were really good at helping talk through anything we needed to with the shock of the poverty and culture change.

That evening we had a house party for the volunteers that were leaving. We decorated by painting our self-portraits onto paper plates and then dressed in our best African outfits with neon face paint, (I do not know who saw this as an essential item to bring with them!) It was one of the best parties I have ever been too!

However we were travelling the next day to Mole National Park which was a ten-hour journey. We thought that if we stayed up partying and booked the taxi at 3am then we would be knocked out for the journey.

The taxi was a small car with mis-matched doors and wooden seats covered in torn fabric. The plan worked and we all just passed out sleeping despite the lack of comfort, and when I woke up I thought we must be halfway there... it had been thirty minutes. After struggling through another three hours, the taxi broke down. The driver thought he had put the wrong fuel into the car which would mean we were completely stranded in a tiny village, you do not get car breakdown services here! We were sitting on the side of the road with the heat of the day setting in as well as the hangovers. We watched the people in the village start their days, which was interesting and kept us going. After an hour, somehow the car started and we all got back in, thank goodness. He started the engine and then... it burst into flames! We grabbed our bags and did a dramatic tuck and roll back out of the car, and now we knew for certain that we were stranded and had no idea what we would do. However this evidently was a very British mentality and this was Ghana, so suddenly everyone ran over to help and started throwing sand into the engine. They continued working on it until they actually managed to start it up again. How they did that I do not know! But we were back in the car starting the next six hours of the journey. Three more hours went by and then we hit what I described as "death road" where it became an incredibly bumpy dirt track and was to be the road for the remainder of the journey, another three hours. Hungover, tightly packed into a car, 40C heat, sitting on wooden seats and going over that kind of road was definitely an endurance test!

You may wonder what we did if and when we needed the toilet, which was inevitable on a ten-hour drive and having been drinking all night. Well, let me tell you... I mentioned I needed the toilet and the driver immediately pulled onto the side of the road, but there was nothing around at all and when he got out of the car I thought he was annoyed and that he was going to shout at me! He went and opened the boot of the car where there was a stock of toilet paper. He threw one my way and pointed through the trees.

I did not mind this after camping several times and now being in Ghana, so strolled into the bushes. Halfway through going for a wee, I heard something and when I looked around, saw a goat staring at me looking as if it were about to charge. Speeding up the process in slight panic, I got up to run and lost my shoe, I managed to pick it up but no time to put it on which resulted in me running out of the bushes to my friends and the driver, with a shoe in one hand and toilet roll unravelling in the other hand. The ones that did not know me were wondering what on earth happened, the ones that did know me looking as if to say, "of course". At least it provided laughter and I got to stretch my legs!

When we did finally arrive we were not in the highest of spirits and I wanted to cry thinking we made a huge mistake, especially as we had to do that journey back in two days! To add to it all, we were told we had to order lunch at breakfast so there was not anything for us to eat. We were absolutely starving, but that is not something we could complain about after what we had experienced volunteering so far. An hour later we found ourselves in a swimming pool drinking beer instead, surrounded by nature with monkeys and elephants roaming around. It was fair to say our moods had now changed slightly, going from rock bottom to feeling on top of the world.

We went to bed early as we were getting up at 6am to go on a walking safari tour. We saw Antelopes, Water Boars, Elephants, Crocodile, and many more amazing animals very closely. It was incredible.

We had remembered to order breakfast the night before so then arrived back to omelettes, toast, jams and nice coffee. This was only our first weekend so though we had not been "deprived" of food and luxuries for long, it felt like we were at a five-star banquet!

When we went back to the pool, we saw a monkey steal someone's bag, we had been told not to bring anything out with us as they were trained to do this and bring it to their owners. When walking around we would see monkeys relaxing at the back of trucks drinking a can of soda they had taken.

Later in our room I opened the front door to a slight surprise shouting to my friend, "there's an elephant at our door." Literally right there in front of my face! He replied, "I'm a bit busy, there are some monkeys at the back." It was all so surreal.

We were told about a canteen near the hotel for lunch. When we got there, it was a tiny shack with one plastic table and a few chairs outside. You did not order, you got what you were given, and this was a huge rice ball in the middle of peanut soup. The idea was to scoop some of the sticky rice with your hand, collecting soup on the way, you did not have cutlery here and this meal was cheap and filling. I loved it! I then went to climb trees, I was evidently in my natural habitat as the year of the Monkey! I was joined by a Ghanaian man and we sat talking for an hour and then he offered to take us all on a canoeing trip down a river. Of course we took him up on this and thought we were going to die when we found ourselves surrounded by crocodiles, rowing through dirty water covered in algae and ducking under trees. We arrived at a local Muslim village which was worth the journey! We saw a mosque built by the community and the straw houses surrounding it which they slept in during the day and then on the roof at night as it was cooler. We explored for a couple of hours and felt very welcome to do so, it was a fascinating cultural and amazing experience.

After an incredible couple of days, we now had the journey back to the house! Well at least it could not get any worse than on the way there…

We broke down 6 times. The driver went another way to avoid the death road and we ended up getting stuck in deep sand instead. We had to dig the car free for an hour in the midday heat, but it was when a fly was buzzing around my head constantly that I got so agitated and started taking all my anger out on the fly by shouting and hitting at it. It is amazing how it is that one little thing that can just push you over the edge and you project all frustration onto. That poor fly...

When we finally got back into the car, we were sweaty, dirty and very uncomfortable with 8 hours to go. That was if the tyre did not then burst five minutes after digging the car free from the sand! The driver changed the tyre which took half an hour and we set off again. I could not believe it when we came to a dead end which meant we had gone the wrong way for an hour, got stuck in sand for no reason and had to go back the same way which risked us getting stuck again! We had no alternative option but luckily, maybe lucky is not the word, we made it through the sand and on the road to begin the journey from the start and tackle death road anyway.

The car was as fed up as us as the battery went flat. The driver again got out to fix it and continued. Then we got a petrol leak. The driver was still not phased and seemed very calm; we were quite the opposite! He managed to fix this as well with what looked like blue-tack mixed with water, again with no option of breakdown rescue, they had to find a way which was a highly respectable and admirable quality. We have too many options to give up or pass the baton to someone else in our first world countries.

For the duration of the journey we had to keep restarting the flat battery and continuously repair the leak, but we had reached the stage of feeling delirious from the heat, exhaustion and petrol fumes so we started to play car games and giggled our way through the nightmare. We made it back, thank goodness! We all jumped up and down hugging each other, including the driver. The other volunteers and staff at the house saw us doing this while covered in dust, sand, dirt and sweat and were just dying to know what on earth happened!!!

After an adventurous weekend, I had signed up to a week of building at the school with two other volunteers. We were building a foundation for a toilet block which is the hardest task with minimal visual outcome, but it was great to take it on so that others would have the incentive to continue the project when we left.

On the first day the head teacher's son asked me to go and get weed killer with him which sounded like a very feasible task. Three hours later...

To get to the local shop to buy building and gardening supplies, we had to walk through a village to get a rowing boat across to Lake Volta. This boat was full of local people who were staring at me with such intensity for the journey, not in an aggressive way but intrigued as to who I was and why I was there. When we arrived, we had another fairly long walk so we stopped at a dodgy looking backstreet "bar" where he bought us soft drinks and then sat to relax. I was eager to be building so I became quite impatient and made him rush, he was also trying to flirt with me which made me very uneasy and anxious with being on my own and now so far from the others.

We finally reached the shop to get the weed killer, I probably could have pulled out all the weeds myself by now! We then had to wait an hour and a half before the boat came to bring us back and it was even busier this time as the locals had bought bags of fish and one man had a goat which was tied by its legs upside down and screaming, it was horrible and I remember this distressing image well. But it was how life was there in poverty.

I finally made it back to do a little bit of building, but most were more intrigued to hear about yet another of my adventures! I am still known today by coming back with a story no matter how small the task I set out to do is.

When I told my sister about it she was so angry with me for going with him. I knew things were not quite as easy to get hold of in Ghana, but I did not expect to have to walk through two villages and get a boat to another island! I would have thought twice if I knew of the adventure to come.

The next day I went straight to where we were building, taking no diversions!

The process was very tiring. We mixed the cement and then put it into small, metal bowls to carry over to where the bricks were being laid. We alternated this with carrying the bricks over to the man who was laying them. He knew how to do this with such precision using a pattern of string, it was very impressive.

When I got out of bed the next day my muscles were so sore and I was very sunburnt, but we were told this day would be a little more relaxed. When we arrived at the school, we found out the reason for that and it was a reason I did not like.

We were beginning to fill the foundation with sand which was the longest process given the size of the bowls we were using, which were very small. But when I say we, the head teacher was in and would not allow us to carry them and made the children do this, some as young as five. We filled them with sand and then they had to carry them on their heads, we were forbidden to do so.

The least I could do was buy them all a bag of water, for which they were so appreciative, but I had to bring an 8-year-old boy to carry it for me.

When we were finished with this stage of building for the day, I began to clean the children's cuts which I had noticed were beginning to become infected, it felt rewarding to be helping them, but more so when seeing their faces at someone caring so much.

I was starting to feel exhausted with the physical and emotional exertion, but I also could not sleep well at night because I now had to be in a tight sleeping bag as there were hundreds of tiny ants over the walls and one morning, I woke up with bites all over my arms as they could get through the mosquito nets. It is incredibly hot and humid at night so it was a debate on which was worse, being wrapped in a sleeping bag or being bitten! It is also possible that the bites from that night were a cause of a blood infection only detected five years later by a research specialist in infectious disease. My abnormal blood test results and other possible symptoms were consistently assumed to be a result of the Anorexia Nervosa, despite my belief in it being something else.

It was day three of building and having had little sleep, I was told this would be the hardest day. They were not lying on that one! But at least without the head teacher around, we were doing the manual labour. We had to loosen the hard sand with a big axe, to then shovel into the metal bowls, carry it over to the foundation and fill the gaps. It was so demoralising seeing how little one bowl covered and felt like a never-ending task. We had Ghanaian men helping us and even they were struggling and needed long breaks, let alone us!

Typically, it was also very muggy but that was soon rectified when the following day we woke up to huge storms and the rain making us freezing cold. We could not continue building and had to try and shelter the children while keeping them warm by singing and dancing. It was also another volunteers last day and when she tried to give out biscuits it turned into a riot of children and the volunteer helpers had to step in to help control the situation. It was literally for one biscuit each but became quite scary with the desperation of each child not wanting to miss out on this rare luxury.

The level of poverty became more obvious to us each day. I offered to help a family out in a local village with two of the other volunteers. The manager of the volunteering company took us, and when we parked, we saw nice-looking houses and we were a bit confused.

He took us down through grass and stinging nettles to get to the tiny wooden shack, which was the family's home. The world is cruel when you could look up above and see the luxury houses.

The shack was about a 15ft (4.5 metres) square which slept 8 of them. There was a one-year-old boy and the mother was seventeen years old. She had sold herself at the age of fifteen for the equivalent of one euro to feed the family for a week. Heart-breaking and shocking.

There was no electricity and there were no windows, so they ate a portion of rice or dough in the morning and a second portion before sundown before they went to bed. Inside there was one dirty mattress for the adults and one for the children.

When I asked what the three ft. square shack was on the side, I was saddened to hear it was the bathroom. They rationed the rainwater between washing in there and for drinking.

I wanted to buy them a house and a new life, but unfortunately we had to obtain the realistic mentality that we could not help them out of such poverty and sadly so many were in the same situation. We therefore decided to buy them bunk beds to fit in the room so they could have four separate beds instead of two. We also bought them a supply of soap, toothbrushes, feminine care products, store cupboard food and colouring books for the children. We also just spent time with them and gave them the priceless gift of human compassion. When we left them on the last visit, they shook our hands and with huge appreciation said, "God bless you". I wish we could have done more.

The following weekend we were staying at our volunteering house. The weekends were hard as we wanted to use them to explore, relax and enjoy ourselves, but after working with such deprived children and visiting slums, there was a guilt looming in the back of our minds.

We did the Saturday morning chore of washing, by which I mean swirling clothes around in the same small bucket we used for a shower. Imagine washing clothing you had been wearing in 45C heat while building in a dusty environment, in one small bucket… I think the last items came out dirtier. We then relaxed sunbathing, but when I opened my eyes I saw local children staring at us bemused. When we asked the staff about it, they said they would have been highly confused as to what we were doing laying IN the sun!

In the afternoon, the leader of the volunteering company took us to get the wood for the bunk beds that would be built for the family we had visited, and then he took us to one of the richest houses in Ghana – one of his friends. There was a tennis court and they invited us to play but we were wearing flop-flops! In true Ghana style, we took our shoes off and played bare feet with rackets they had lying around. It was a surreal experience, but again felt so wrong to be on the grounds of someone so rich, while surrounded by the worst poverty. These houses were also mainly for show and the owners would often live elsewhere or be travelling between their many houses, how is that fair? I wish this wealth could be split amongst the poor for everyone to have a quality of life.

The following day we went out on a boat at a lake with locals from the village. The water was incredibly dirty, but it was too hot to resist going for a swim! When we looked back at the boat, we saw the locals scooping the water into bottles to drink! We were horrified and tried to explain about it making them unwell and precautions to take, but they would not believe us and said that it was the cleanest water they drank.

We were then taken to a waterfall where I had the best shower! I have never felt so clean after two weeks of showering with a bucket. When we arrived home the staff had cooked us dinner, for which we paid, and was possibly the nicest meal I had ever tasted. It was a simple delight of chicken and rice which is considered a lean and boring meal in out western lifestyle and had when there is nothing else in the cupboard, but here it was the most luxurious meal. The most amazing part was having actual chicken meat on the chicken which they would have spent a long time trying to find at a very high cost! We were without power again that evening so resumed the drinking games by candlelight, singing and dancing. The feeling of happiness was overwhelming from the most simplistic of days.

For my third week at the school, I started teaching alongside another volunteer as I was going to take her class on my own for my last week when she leaves.

We began with math and I noticed one boy around the age of 8 was not understanding or following, I was told by the other children and teachers to just leave him, but I took him aside to try and help him. We began doing simple counting and sums but the "real" teachers, were hitting him on the head while laughing and calling him stupid. I was so angry but also came to realise I was powerless; this is how it was for them and no temporary volunteer would change that or take that power from them.

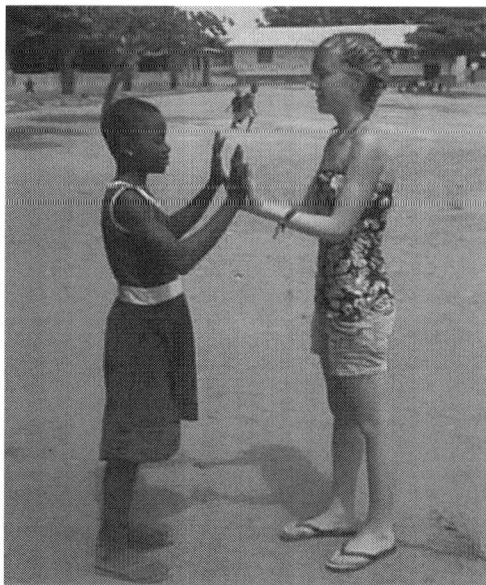

The children do not have a school psychologist, a counsellor or a support group to turn to, they may not have even had a family to do so.

On the days that these "real" teachers taught, they would repeat the exact same class, teaching the same short story and same eight mathematical sums, while walking around threatening them with the cane. I was more terrified than they were of them using it, and also at the thought of how many years they had sat through that one class.

That evening, all the volunteers went to a local village to install one of the first water filters for clean drinking water. We brought juice, rice and biscuits along with other small gifts for them all as it was to be a celebration.

When we drove through the flooded dirt tracks, we saw a group jumping and cheering with excitement as we arrived.

I had expected a slight riot at trying to hand out the gifts after experiencing this at the school, but we all sat in a circle and were welcomed with prayers and words of thanks. At the end of this we were given a shot of their local alcohol that they made, which was 60% in strength! We went around one-by-one being watched by everyone, trying to keep a straight face while the fireball went down your throat. Somehow we had a few more later on and went home very drunk!

After the words of thanks and prayers, we presented the water filter and showed them how it worked. When they were passing the clean water around, their faces were of such happiness and shock that we were all in tears.

The celebration continued with the gifts being given out and we started to disperse and talk amongst the locals. A small boy, around the age of two, came to sit on my lap and he stayed there for three hours, so calm and quiet, just wanting some attention and affection. He had the bloating of malnourishment as well as the yellowing in his

eyes and I remember him well to this day, wondering if he is ok, wishing I could have taken him back with me.

Everyone was so overwhelmed, an experience and feeling I will never be able to fully describe, but the memories from it are still so clear in my mind.

At the weekend, a few of us decided on a weekend away to a beach resort called "Krokobite", this time the journey was just three hours long, much better than the previous weekend away which was 10 hours! But when we had travelled for two hours and asked how long was left, we were shocked when the driver told us another four hours! We were in the same style car as with the other journey, sitting on wooden seats, going over dirt tracks and with a full car during the heat of the day. It always ends up being worth it and no matter how stressful the journey, you cannot help but be calm and smile when arriving at these amazing destinations. We arrived to a show and a party on the beach before being shown to our little beach hut. We decided to opt out of having air conditioning to save money, which was a really bad idea with it being sweltering heat in the huts during the night! It was more of a holiday style resort, so we got to order breakfast which was pure luxury, and then went to the beach to relax, sunbathe and swim in the sea. Though unfortunately the water was so rough that we could only manage to get in about knee depth before being completely wiped out... it was quite funny for both us and spectators! Going back to the hut to get ready for the evening, we found that the first running shower we would have had was broken! We were all looking forward to this shower so much that it hurt to find this out. When we asked if they could fix it, they shouted at us saying it was not their fault, and after much persuasion, they kindly allowed us to use buckets to have bucket showers... at least we were used to this. We all made an effort to dress up for the evening when we were going to an actual restaurant to eat an actual meal! Then we went to a beach party, however, we were a group of white girls and this caused us to get harassed quite a lot and became too much, so we all went back to the beach hut and relaxed there.

To be honest, I was quite bored during the weekend. I remember the location and it would have ordinarily been such a great weekend, but with all that we had experienced in Ghana and all the adventures, a beach weekend was just, dull!

An hour into the journey back to the volunteer house, I needed the toilet, and driving along dirt tracks made it hard to hold. I did not want to go on the side of the road in fear of another goat incident, but I could not handle five more hours, so I asked the driver. Thank goodness I did as out of nowhere we pulled into an actual service station with shops, restaurants and flushing toilets with toilet paper and soap dispensers. We were ridiculously excited and spent a while in the services, not quite understanding how or why they were there! It made the rest of the journey a lot easier having had such a luxurious stop and feeling quite baffled by it as well.

For my last week, I was teaching my own class and I was both excited and nervous. I was proud of how I managed and it was such a huge sense of achievement when successfully teaching how to tell the time, label shapes, do maths and create sentences, especially when the children were so grateful to be learning.

During the break, a boy named Isaac who was aged 9, wanted me to meet his family at his home in the village. He had helped me throughout my stay in Ghana and was very mature. Though the building was a roughly laid brick wall with a metal roof and no flooring but the natural sand, there was space and he had his own room. Having been to those even less fortunate I was pleasantly surprised, but if I had seen this at the beginning of my stay I would have been horrified. It was both amazing and sad how accustomed you became to how their lives were.

His father was a fisherman and showed me the bucket of fish he had caught that day while the younger brother sliced them, and the mother cooked them. Only one child could go to school as they could not afford to send both and needed one to help with the life chores. They were cooking the fish heads to eat themselves as they needed to sell the good meat, the smell was incredibly pungent and the fish looked as though they had gone slightly rotten. So when the mother asked me to stay and have this lunch with them, I did not know what to do as this was the most loving and incredible offer to be given, to be offered their rationed food, but the sight and the smell was so horrific. I said that I had to get back to teach at the school, and thankfully she gave them to me to take away. I walked back to the school with three rotten fish heads in a bag which was now being swarmed with flies. I ran to the minibus driver and told him what had happened, he was laughing uncontrollably and took them from me to eat very quickly in front of me for his lunch. A delicacy.

We had another house party that evening, singing and dancing until 1am... the 7am start was not the most pleasant the next day! I was luckily showing a new volunteer my class which meant having help and at one point, the children were using fans to cool me down as I laid on a bench. Teacher of the year! Also, to the outsider looking in, so morally wrong! Luckily we all knew it was a fun and trusting relationship, the children had learnt that the volunteers were not wanting to be "served" and it meant they could relax and be cheeky kids.

Making up for my dire start to the day, I took Isaac and his friend to a space to teach them Tennis with the rackets I brought over with me. A group of girls from the school followed and so I taught them all and was so proud when they began to hit the ball well, we even managed to play a proper tennis match, teaching them how to score.

Though there was no net or court laid out, when the crowd began to gather, it put The Wimbledon Championships to shame! I decided to let them keep these tennis rackets so that they could continue playing together and be children for a while. That was the idea anyway, until I found that Isaac had been chased and beaten to get the racket from him which he was incredibly reluctant to give up. The guilt of this, the image of it, still stays with me to this day.

The following day was my last day at the school. I woke up so early in disbelief that such an incredible experience was coming to an end. I would not wake up to cornflakes and powdered milk before climbing into a crammed minibus with our driver Kwasi. I would not spend the day at Sunrise school and would be leaving those children behind.

I was going to miss the simplicity of life with the evenings filled with tasks for basic life necessities. Filling a bucket for a shower, cleaning clothes by hand, cooking noodles by candlelight, and then sitting around talking with one another while playing games. No phones, no signal, no laptops, no television. Bliss.

I brought sweets in for the class I had been teaching and one of the girls wanted to take me to meet her family before I left. I felt incredibly honoured as she was not the easiest of children and had no trust in people, refusing to ever let anyone near her house. I remember Josephine, wearing Christmas pyjamas each day with no idea that the image on them was of snowmen or even what snow was. Her family laughed and joked with me about our vastly different lives, but I felt embarrassed at all I had.

We drove back from the school and I was inevitably crying throughout the journey.

On my last evening, a huge storm came at 11:30pm and so we grabbed our shampoo for our natural and most amazing outdoor shower! I was so happy that this happened on my last night, truly dancing in the rain.

When the taxi arrived the next morning, I could not hold it together and was in floods of tears. I had been through an experience of a lifetime and after the battles beforehand, it was even more incredible. I had not told anyone about suffering from anorexia, nor did anyone suspect anything, I was just Rachael for a month.

I was not going home quite yet though, I was meeting my friend who travelled with me in Accra, he had gone a few days earlier. My Dad offered to pay for a hotel for us to stay in, but I had managed the month on my own and would not accept the offer. We ended up staying in the cheapest hostel in the capital of Ghana. Possibly a slight mistake...

We went for a walk but felt uneasy so thought it was best to go back to our room. However, on our way back we found a bar which ended up being our place of safety and respite for the next couple of days! They ended up knowing us well and our drinks order, bringing them as soon as we arrived before even sitting down... Eclipse bar, our absolute saviour!

After a few drinks at Eclipse the first evening, we went back to the hostel and played mini golf in the tiny hostel room. I wish I could tell you where we found the mini clubs and ball, but I have absolutely no idea!

The next day we could not stay around the area, so we decided to locate a nice beach, tourist attraction or not, we were going! We started walking and when we came across a market, I innocently went in to get a banana. Everyone seemed to stop and stare at us, and then one lady starting to shout in another language "GO!", while shooing us away... it was slightly terrifying and I am not sure what line we crossed!

While desperately trying to find a taxi, we walked past the other side of the market where the stench of rotten fish was over-powering and we had to quickly dodge a girl who was going for a poo right in the middle of the pavement. She was very relaxed about it, as were all the others walking around.

We jumped in the first taxi we found to take us to the beach. When we started seeing luxury homes and tourist shops, I hate to say I felt such relief. We stepped onto a gorgeous beach and were shown to sun-loungers. I could not help but indulge in the absolute bliss of it all and enjoyed a refreshing mango juice with a delicious lunch.

However, when I went into the sea, two men started pulling my ankles down under the waves. They were doing it in what was thought to be a "fun and flirty" way, but it was by no means fun for me and was incredibly terrifying. My friend had to run in to pick me up and get out of the sea with me... I spent the rest of the afternoon on the sand!

Back at the hostel, the shower was shared, cold and dirty... but it felt like luxury! We went to a posh restaurant to treat ourselves as the experience in Ghana was about come to an end. One I will ensure never to forget as we both felt uncomfortable in this "upper class" environment after the month's experience and it felt wrong. So we ate quickly and went back to Eclipse bar for our final drinks!

I had been nicknamed Rocky over my stay in Ghana with no shame in saying I held my head high with this. I was, and still am, incredibly proud of my strength over that month after all that had happened. No matter what came after it, I will remain safe in the knowledge that it was the best decision of my life.

6

Working in France

I had lost weight in Ghana which was not unexpected as everyone did due to the way in which we were living, and I was actually really pleased and relieved that this had not caused "Rex" to take over my mind again. My parents had lived through the anorexia with me and they also saw that my mental state was positive and stable, but they insisted I should go to the doctor for a check-up which was understandable.

I saw the doctor that I had seen when I initially went with my self-diagnosis, the same one that said I was fine and it was just "a phase". This time she did not listen to what I had to say once again but reverted to her shouting at me for losing weight, purposely relapsing and making me feel guilty by reminding me how much my parents had spent for me to go to the private clinic. She called my therapist and my Mum to say I looked gaunt and like a walking skeleton. As this came from a doctor, everyone reacted with her and would not listen to me or the fact that I had been in Ghana. I was not given any time to build myself back up, though I had asked for a steak dinner upon return, my label was "Anorexic" and that would not be forgotten.

I was taken to the nurses' office for urgent blood tests while having a screaming match with the doctor, causing a slight scene!

I felt like a sane person in an insane place. When I had told people I was struggling at the beginning, they would not listen, said I was fine, and sent me on my way to continue my life. Now I felt well in my mind but I LOOKED thin, I was misunderstood and not listened to again.

That is the issue with mental health, if it is not visible people cannot understand it. There was not a set prescription or a cure, so it was ignored until there were physical symptoms to address instead.

I was supposed to be going to France for the summer to work as a children's courier at a holiday resort a week later and was told by the doctor I had the week to prove myself, but if I did not gain weight, I would not be going.

I did everything I could by drinking build up shakes and eating a high calorie diet, so when I went back a week later, I was in disbelief that I had lost weight. I had taken a food diary with me to show what I had eaten over the week and my dad was with me who had witnessed this as the truth. But the scales had spoken, the doctor would not listen to us and I was told I was lying. I felt like a criminal.

My Dad was also in disbelief, so we asked for different scales and to use the same ones I had been weighed on the previous week. When we convinced her to allow us to do this, the scales showed I had gained 3kg (6.5lb)! It became a type of show with Dad and the doctor trying both sets of scale as well, proving that they had a 2-3kg (4.5-6.5lb) difference.

Now that the numbers were different, I was treated like a human being again and given the chance to have a conversation as a person, not a number. However she decided that the difference in scales would balance out as having maintained my weight and told me I could not go to France.

Obviously I was fuming by the way I was treated and the situation with the scales, so I told her exactly what I thought and that she would have to send an army to the airport to stop me from going to France.

Through my rage and shouting, all she could say in response was, "it would be against medical advice". It was also against the advice of my Mum which hurt much more to defy. She knew it was not going to end well for me, but she also knew that she would not be able to change my mind or to stop me either.

Four days later, I left for the West Mediterranean.

France was another incredible experience. Though very different to Ghana, it was continuing to live life in a simplistic way. My house for the summer was a tent, I would cycle down to the on-site bakery to get a fresh croissant each morning and have to cycle to the nearest toilet and shower (not fun if you needed the toilet in the night!) I took part in the evening entertainment which was foam parties, drinking, dancing and even doing our own act on stage. I ran a children's club in the morning and the evening, in between I had some work for the apprenticeship we got while there but ultimately enjoyed the sun, swimming pool, beaches and life!

The night I arrived I was asked within minutes if I wanted to go to a night-time theme park and that they had saved me a seat. So I threw my suitcase into the tent I was sharing and off I went! It was very surreal to be going around a loud, vibrant theme park with a group of people I did not know existed that morning.

We went to big festivals, watched movies on an outdoor screen and the best thing that happened was when they had made an error with the accommodation, ultimately resulting in me without a tent! So they put one up in a random patch and I lived with a French girl who spoke minimal English. It has always been an ambition of mine to learn French and I studied it to A-level but could never become confident in speaking it. After that summer, I could speak conversational fluent French and spent most of my time with the French groups, it was fantastic! When my sister and parents came to visit, I naturally switched to French when speaking with these friends and I felt so proud of it.

However, the demon in my mind began to return and it became stronger and stronger because my weight continued to decline. I could not understand as I was overcoming a lot with five-course meals, barbecues, crepes, ice creams and croissant but I could see I was losing weight and I knew with each pound I lost, "Rex" became fiercer. Yet I felt powerless to change anything as I did not know what to change as I was genuinely doing the same as everyone else, but they did not become incredibly underweight so something must have been wrong. It was highlighted years later that it may have been due to the blood infection I had picked up in Ghana but did not yet know about. So I have described an amazing summer, but the reality is, a lot of the time I was in despair with segregation due to this torment. I felt lonely, fearful and confused but was losing weight rapidly and struggling with the physical exertion of each day in the heat.

When my parents came to visit, they saw the dramatic drop and it was not pleasant for any of us. My Mum was upset and angry for the duration of their stay and we ended in many tears when I refused to go home with them when my mum was adamant that I did.

If I went back with my parents I would have ended up in hospital, if I stayed for another month, I would also end up in hospital, so I had to enjoy as much as I could. I had a month left of freedom. I knew that.

My eldest sister came in the last week and I warned her I did not look good. The morning she arrived we went for coffee and breakfast. She said she was shocked and scared when she saw me but seeing me at such ease eating and smiling made her less concerned.

That was my dilemma too, the illness was becoming more complex, more cryptic, making it harder for us all to understand and fight it.

In that final week, we did not have any children's clubs as it was the end of the summer, so we were all asked to clean the mobile homes, the tents, the cabins and the pathways. It was hard work. I was finding it too much physically and was worrying at losing even more weight before going home, so I had to tell the manager that I could not do this work and told her everything about my anorexia. When I shared with her about the battles I was facing, she was shocked as said I did not stop eating and seemed so happy. This was again infuriating as it looked like I had eaten nothing all summer and that is what everyone would believe when they saw me.

When I went to the airport to fly home with my sister, I burst into tears with pure fear. My jeans were falling down and I had to hold them up or they would have been around my ankles. I messaged my parents to warn them and the response being that my Mum wanted to run away as she did not think she could face seeing it.

I was going to be put into hospital, maybe even sectioned. I knew it. I was panicking.

My sister calmed me down and told me it would all be ok. Wrong.

When I arrived home, it should have been excitement, stories, showing photos and catching up with everyone, but I do not think I showed a single photo or told a story for the first two weeks. I was quickly whisked away to see the doctor urgently due to my low weight. When I came downstairs in a pair of jeans and a long sleeve white top to go to the doctor, Mum told me to go and put a jumper on because people were going to stare at me. I remember that outfit, I remember how I looked. I knew I was skeletal, but I was able to eat well and I felt well in my mind. On my first day back I had pancakes for brunch and a roast dinner in the evening and I was so happy with eagerness to tell people about my time away.

I did not understand what had happened or what is happening.

I was banned from all physical activity, driving and even from going to the shop. My Mum bought me scrap booking equipment, so I did this each day for my time in Ghana and France. When she arrived home with it and I went to the car to help her unload, I was told I was not allowed to carry a thing and to get back inside.

I was being treated as critically ill, though I had not been asked how I was mentally, which at this point did not match my body. It was a role reversal and I remember wishing that my mind and body would match for once, whether that was unwell or healthy. I wish I could have taken this back as I began to enter the mental torment of anorexia as the voice returned and the decline was vicious. It told me I did not get ill enough last time, but this time I would. The mischievous ways began with hiding food, throwing it

away, water on cereal, cutting out the middle of a bread roll so people did not see and thought it was a full sandwich, and so many more tricks that felt on autopilot as they were dictated to me. My therapist at the time saw my deterioration, I was always very honest with my therapists. I told her I no longer believed that anorexia could be beaten, that I would follow its voice until the end, it was easier this way.

No matter how deep into this mentality, that glimmer of Rachael always remained and I knew I did want to be free, I needed intense help. I wanted to go back to the clinic I was at before, but I would not ask my parents to fund this again, and I would need to stay for much longer. If I told them this, they would also feel guilty that they could not fund me to go and worry that I was basically saying "I can't do this without it." So again I took it into my own hands to try and get the funding granted for the help I needed.

I went back to the doctor's clinic, but I could not and would not see the doctor who had been overseeing my care thus far as she would have sectioned me, so when I explained to the new doctor about everything, she nodded along and then did the protocol of weighing me. Only then did she say, "oh my goodness you are tiny". Yes, I have just told you I have anorexia, would you LOOK at me as a person not a statistic? Would you just listen to me? The doctor agreed to do her best to get this funding for me and that she would ring in two days. I was very tense and the most anxious for those two days I had ever been. I felt I had to be even more sneaky and restrict as if I gained any weight, I would have less chance of being granted this funding for hospital. Sadly, this was not my interpretation, it genuinely was the way the system worked, and I could not even confide in my parents as they did not know about it.

Two days later, the doctor called me and said, "no can do with funding, sorry, good luck."

I wrote to the clinic in Norwich, which was painful to do having been such a "miracle" in my stay there before and now having to tell them how bad things become. As caring as they are, they are still stuck in the same system and could not help if the doctors did not grant funding.

I researched other means of help and found a centre which helped you to learn to cope with life, stress and the mental side of anorexia as opposed to just re-feeding, but I was not in the correct geographical area zone to be accepted.

One of my last options was a week programme with therapy groups and supported eating two days a week. It was better than nothing.

When I contacted them, I was told I would have to apply to go back to my outpatient team, then be accepted onto their day patient treatment that I had previously attended, to then be transferred to this programme. The process taking approximately one year.

Having had a bad experience with the day patient programme and having deteriorated further there, it was not an option and a ridiculous system at that.

So here was a suffering anorexic, crying out for help and wanting treatment, and all the doors being shut in my face.

Exhausted. Worn down. Becoming defeated.

During the search for support, my health was rapidly declining, so I had another appointment with another doctor. My sister came with me and we told the doctor that I had just been for a big lunch with her, so despite my BMI now at fourteen, she said as I seemed energetic and was managing to eat, I should just carry on.

While I made this effort to defeat the demons in my mind, it made them angry at me and they started their retaliation.

"Can't you see that no-one cares". "Would they not give you help if you needed it?". "You don't deserve the help."

I was also feeling angry towards my parents and started to think that they were exaggerating how unwell I was so they could just stop me from leaving again. This shows the strength of this illness, as if it could make me believe this about my parents, it could make me believe anything.

The demons had won and I now believed I was fine, so I stopped searching for help and I returned to work at the theatre and at a coffee shop. It also helped me to cope with each day.

Christmas was coming around again, and I had been working a lot. I was back in the same turmoil with feeling as though I needed to lose more weight to get help, but my parents were still unaware that I had been trying to get it, how many times I had been turned away, and that the voice was in my head again. Louder than ever.

That is until Christmas Day came and after an argument, I completely broke down and told them everything.

They held me tight, all the animosity leaving and we became a strong team again. A huge relief.

We all began researching how beat these demons. They found new research into The Insular Cortex of the brain and how this may be playing a part in my illness and the reason I could not seem to get better no matter how much I tried. Damage to The Insular Cortex can be a result of hypoxia, starvation of oxygen to the brain, which I endured on the ski trip just before anorexia began.

It was a boost that I needed after being accused by medical professionals that I did not want to get better, that I was using laxatives, making myself sick and ultimately playing games. This was something that showed that it was not my fault and was such a relief that for that moment, I was not to blame.

Unfortunately, with this being new research, we were not getting any further with it and doctors again were telling us we were "clutching at straws". Thank goodness for my parents and how they did not take this same mentality but stood right by my side the whole time with full trust and faith in me. They would help me find a way.

My application for funding had finally been put to the authorities, but as it was Christmas, we were told the meeting would not be for another month. A torturous wait, but there was a date to work towards and we came together to get through it with games and movies, but there was limited entertainment for someone who could not enjoy food and drink and was not well enough for physical exertion. The days were hard.

The date we were working towards finally came, and then it went. We heard nothing. A few more days passed when we were told the meeting had been postponed but was being held at that moment and we would be called the next day. That day came and went. I could not do this anymore. I was not sure if my body could either. Weekends were the worst as we could not call anyone to find out any information, usually people love the weekends, but we dreaded them and felt alone.

I was both physically and mentally declining, I was now obsessed with lowering my daily calorie intake each day and was using an app on my phone to know the exact amount of nutrition for every single thing I consumed. More tricks were being invented with things like buying medium eggs and putting them in the "large" egg box because at that time, that mattered. I tore the middle of a slice of bread out and filled the hole with spinach so that the crust was seen, and my parents would think I had a large egg on toast. I left wrappers on the side counters to look as though I had eaten a snack and making sure that the actual snack was broken into little pieces and put into other bits of rubbish in the bin to ensure it was never found.

I was doing secret exercise at every possible minute that I could, though my parents could not leave me for long. I would do jumping jacks, run up and down the stairs, and whatever else my mind created for me to do. This got more compulsive each time and I would be willing my parents to come back home so that I could stop.

I managed to stay away from ever making myself sick with having a huge fear and hatred of it, though it had often entered my mind. I am not sure my body or mind would have coped with that as well. I did however try laxative tea and I vowed I never would again! I was in the most horrific amount of pain and really did not think my body was going to cope through it with being at such a low body weight with little substance inside me as it was. I did not think it would have that much of an effect!

My weight was dropping each week and now other symptoms were beginning. The dentist said that I was risking losing my adult teeth because my gums were in such poor health. I had sores on my skin, my hair was falling out and my circulation was non-existent. I looked like the walking dead.

I knew that even when I put all of my strength into fighting anorexia at home, my mind was too strong and now that my weight was so low, I feared putting any of it back on to be seen as physically managing but left with the demons.

I hate to say, that I think it was the right thing to do with finally getting the phone call that I had received funding! The relief was immense.

However, we were told that the clinic was now full and we had to wait to be called when a bed was available. So those long days and the waiting game began all over again.

A few days later, to my disbelief, I was watching a programme on diets as I had become obsessed with these as well, and clinic I wanted to be back in and was waiting for came on the show to say how supportive they were of patients struggling with Anorexia, holding their hands and saying, "it is ok not to be ok". I do not think I had ever cried so much at this point with the raw pain of how much I just wanted that help, and my parents also broke down in tears when I showed them this.

The patients on the programme were those I had been with during my short admission and were deeply engrained in anorexia. I had been their inspiration and said to have given them hope, but now the roles were reversed. I was deeply engrained, knocking on deaths' door and inspired by how far they had come in recovery. I was incredibly happy and proud of them, but it made me upset to think I could be free now if I too had the funding to stay there for as long as I needed to. I had fought every single day; I could not understand how or why things had got so bad.

A new month came, it was now February and the only enlightenment to a bed becoming available was that a few patients were in the stage of planning their discharge date. This helped to know that maybe soon… maybe. I was scared, I now truly feared for my life, but I also had the intense fear of my mind which "Rex" now completely dominated.

When we still had not heard that a bed would be available soon, we had to look for an alternative.

I was calling many centres, Eating Disorder Unit co-ordinators, General Co-ordinators, anything that may have some means of support. I was told they would call back or send information and that was all, despite me telling them about my desperate situation and crying for their help.

I had even proposed an idea to the private clinic about beginning a "pre-admission plan" where I could speak to a therapist once a week and start a recovery plan. In my mind, this may allow me the permission to not decline further. However, it was not procedure and could not be done.

I began shouting in the house, screaming that no-one gives a s***. Ironically, it was also Eating Disorders Awareness Week and everything on television and radio was for people to talk and seek support, to which I would scream back, "I AM TRYING!" Media versus reality.

We finally heard from clinic and told there was not a planned discharge until April, with no exact date. Originally it was going to be mid-February so for all we knew, this could be pushed to May, and beyond. My BMI was now at thirteen, there was no option to wait that long.

My Mum was a paramedic at the time and asked for support from her colleagues with my situation. One of them had gone to someone battling Anorexia Nervosa and told her about a unit in London to treat Eating Disorders.

I called them and was passed from person to person before reaching a voicemail to leave a message. I would now have to wait for a reply after the weekend, another weekend to get through. Dad just held my hand as I cried.

When they called back, they asked for my name, e-mail address and my BMI to send me information. My BMI. No how are you in yourself Rachael? How are you feeling? No, my BMI. This again reinforced me that I needed to keep my weight low to get this help. After getting clinical information, I was told they would phone me back again. I waited for four days before I rang them. I was told they were needing to get paperwork to prove I had funding before I could visit the unit or find out any more information.

Though my hopes were diminishing, I kept searching and found another centre for treating addictions and a unit for anorexia nearby. When I called I was expecting the same reaction, but to my surprise the woman was very caring and though she said she would have to have the admission department call me, she ended with "hang in there, everything will be ok", which caused me to cry once again. That is all I had asked for, even if the system had to be followed, just a little care and compassion while helping me find somewhere for treatment. When I was called back, they said I was not eligible as I was too underweight for their programme!!!

I went to my friends' house, she said I looked exhausted and had never seen me look so bad, exhausted and defeated. I curled up on her bed while we just sat in silence and she stroked my hair in comfort, what else could we do or say? Until she came out with the sudden decision that I was to go to the London unit the next day in person and take a stand. I told my parents this and they were in complete agreement, so that is what we did.

Having been in such a homely environment in my previous admission, it was a shock to enter such a clinical environment and to think of it being where I would live. The ward only had six patients on it and it did not seem like a bad option in my condition.

I was handed a huge booklet of information, two-thirds of which were the rules around food and the diet. That was not a good sign to help me with the psychological side I needed.

One rule was that there was a thirty-minute timer and when that went off at the end of the meal, cutlery was to be put down and anything left was weighed out and calculated to be given as a Fort sip supplement shake. It felt like a punishment regime where you were not allowed to struggle and not asked why you struggled with that meal. It did not seem to recognise that anorexia was a mental illness and that the issue with food and weight was a symptom. But, a bed was available.

On the way home, we all felt very down knowing that we knew we would have to take that bed, though it was not going to be a nice experience at all, it would at least save my life. When we got home, we called the funding centre to transfer this to the London unit. As this was about to be finalised, we had an e-mail from clinic we had been waiting for to tell us that a bed would be available for me at the end of the month. A guardian angel was looking over us.

You would think we would have accepted this straight away, but the thought of how we would get through three weeks was so traumatising that we still nearly went for the London unit. But after deliberating, we decided we would work hard and stay strong as a team to get me to the clinic in Norwich. We knew it was a place that had care and compassion, psychological treatment and the chance for a full recovery and to have a decent future. I remember my Mum saying the sentence, "we have to make a plan together to keep you alive for three weeks."

But the deception continued, the secrets, the compulsive actions driven by "Rex". I was unable to eat much at all, exercising to extremes and all the while desperate to stop, but could not. My parents continued their lives, rightly so, but this made "Rex" angry and our relationship became more strained as I found it incredibly difficult to watch Mum and Dad go to play Tennis, clean, work and go out to meetings when I had no aim for the day and being told to stay as still as possible. I can now see why I had to as I was very unwell, but at the time I could only see red and it made my actions worse. People were trying to help me through these weeks as best they could and I went to the cinema with a friend. It was cold for me in there and I had not eaten a lot as I was to be sitting down for a couple of hours to watch the movie, so I brought a small lollipop to help me through

it. However I became breathless, my chest became so tight and my body started shaking. I was incredibly frightened that this was it and made a mental prayer to let me live through the movie and then I would eat something. When I got home and felt a bit better, I ate nothing.

The final week before my admission came and it was set to be a good one as it was also Dad's birthday. It had been agreed by my family that if I ate what was prescribed for me, then I could go to London with my family to watch a West End show at the theatre. I only have vague memories of that show.

We then had more stress with yet more issues with paperwork for my admission and my Dad had to spend a lot of time on the phone once again. They said it was incomplete and I needed to have an approval from Farnham Hospital, where I was four years ago! Firstly, how is that useful when my situation is evidently quite different four years down the line? And also, WHY were we being told this on the Friday before my admission when there were no available doctors at Farnham Hospital to sort this out until Monday? ANOTHER weekend of the waiting game, praying, hoping.

At the doctors, my weight had dropped to 30kg (66lb), a BMI of 12 and we had lost the bed in the London unit, if I could not be admitted to the clinic soon, the next thing to be lost was my life.

In the hope of my admission going ahead, the weekend was full of goodbyes to my friends and family. I would not see much of them with it being four hours away. The care shown, the compassion and the heart-felt hugs from everyone was overwhelming. But a good friend said to me, when she hugged me at that moment, she did not know what kind of goodbye she was saying.

7

The Second Inpatient Admission

"I'm here, finally here. I can crumble, meltdown and show the heartache. I can be fragile. I don't have to battle through every dreaded minute of every dreaded day, I can allow myself to be taken care of."

A bed finally became available for me to be admitted to the clinic in Norwich for the second time. I do not remember the journey there, but my parents do. It was a four-hour drive and they said I collapsed in the back of the car with a blanket over me and they had to keep checking on me in fear that I would not survive the journey. My body was very weak and so stressed that taking the sigh of relief may have been taking a last breath. But I made it and Dad had to carry me to the door of the clinic.

I do remember when I was inside the door as I hung my head in shame of how badly I had relapsed, how awful I looked and not wanting the staff to see the horrific deterioration having left so full of life and healthy two years before. No longer the star patient giving hope of recovery but showing the reality and strength of anorexia.

I had my psychological assessment and it really brought to light the fight I had ahead. I was in a vastly different position to my previous admission, much deeper into the illness, it had a tighter grip on me and very physically unwell. I was terrified of the battle to come. When it came to saying goodbye to my parents, there were no words after everything we had been through together in my deterioration and keeping me alive. The pain in our eyes when they connected said it all.

I had to start on quarter portions which is due to re-feeding syndrome. It is a serious risk when starting to eat and gain weight from such a low BMI and so must be gradually increased from a very small amount while being monitored via blood tests.

These portions were tiny. A bowl of soup being 100ml with ¼ of a bread roll, a jacket potato was a new potato with a teaspoon of tuna, having a quarter of a sandwich. I sometimes felt so hungry as I was used to filling up on such low calorie foods but making it look like more for my parents, whereas now I was having more calorie dense food with the volume being far less. I felt so guilty for feeling hungry, like a fraud. However, I was not to be fooled, I knew how much this increased and I knew within a month I would be on the incredibly high weight gaining diet once more.

The other patients were lovely and most were further along in their admissions, though the eating behaviours were still terrible. People eating sandwiches with knives and forks, pulling it apart to eat every ingredient separately, taking hours to eat a meal. There was a patient who sat at the table all day as it took her so long to eat a meal, it ran into the next snack and meal like a conveyer belt of food. Eating Disorders manifest in many controlling ways. I did not have these behaviours and continued to eat normally, though sometimes I would take hours depending on the trauma I was feeling inside my mind.

My first statement was about the relief of being able to give in and be taken care of. However, waking up the next morning I instinctively rolled down to the side of my bed to do exercise. It was done without any thought at all, just natural. Controlled. After being weighed and getting dressed, I did yet more squats in the toilet. This would now be a cycle I would find near impossible to break but only escalate to extremes. It was incredibly stressful to find where to do the exercise and not be caught. It is one thing being deceptive at my parents' house, it is another with trained staff around 24/7 and fellow eating disorder patients. I also felt defeated as I thought I would get the relief at not having to put myself through this secret exercise anymore. I was not allowed upstairs or even in the garden so I am not even sure myself how I managed to do so much! The power of determination, "Rex" found ways and those ways became more and more deceiving and dangerous. I convinced myself that I would do it for now to help me cope and then slowly wean off it or confess to staff to help me stop. In reality that was never going to happen or be allowed by the demons.

Deciding what to wear on my first morning also turned into an event. I wanting to wear baggy clothes to be hidden, but the other patients looked gorgeous and loved their fashion having been through their admission, so I felt I wanted to dress nicely as well and fit in with them, but that was not going to be possible at this point.

In my first admission, I could not decide what to wear because I felt huge and envied the patients that were "worse" than me, this time I was in turmoil with feeling disgustingly skinny and ashamed, envying the girls looking stunning. There is no winning with this illness. Choosing what to wear in the morning became so distressing for me that it became a part of my care plan to have staff help me choose each morning and support me.

It was time for my first, tiny breakfast and when I went into the lounge for post-meal supervision, I crumbled to my knees with my head in my hands, crying uncontrollably. Another image I find hard to ever forget.

I was then taken to the local doctor for blood tests and in the taxi my head was pounding with a headache and I was so exhausted that I could not keep my eyes open. A staff member I had so much fun with and was really close to in my last admission was with me, and I remember hearing her say to the driver in such sympathy, "she is so exhausted bless her, it is so sad."

I was confused. I felt lost. I felt wrong. Everything felt wrong. I could not talk to anyone because I could not find words to describe how I was feeling, I did not know. All I knew was that I did not want to feel this way, I desperately wanted to be better, but no means of distraction would stop my head shouting at me and feeling in utter turmoil every single minute of the day.

"I really have absolutely zero mental energy now. To even break down and cry, to talk, to even chew and eat. I am completely trapped in my head. When I read, sleep, watch a film… it is all consuming. It is horrific, claustrophobic and I just want a release. Even for 10 minutes. Please."

The first group I had was on Body Image, which was what I related to and found the most useful last time, but this time it was not yet an issue. It had gone far deeper and surpassed body image. But now I did not know what the issue was. It made no sense, none of it made sense as to why I was this way.

I began to develop, or realise, that I felt I deserved to be punished. When my meals were incorrectly portioned and they gave me less than I should have had, my mind said, "see, you shouldn't be getting better, you don't deserve to, they don't even want you to." The amount I had to fight to get into a hospital also became a sign that I did not deserve recovery or help.

Yet I continued writing why I needed to fight it, everything I had to live for and everyone who cared for me and loved me. The element of determination always remained throughout.

"I'm feeling so on edge all of the time, I don't know when I'm going to be set off and taken over by "Rex".

The anxiety of knowing that I was in the complete possession and power of "Rex" was indescribably terrifying. I no longer recognised myself, I snapped at people constantly with anger, I would not smile and I would not talk to anyone because there were no longer any words for the way I felt.

"I did not think I could feel any more exhausted, but I feel like death. I am so cold and can barely write from shaking. My hair feels limp and horrible, my skin is drawn, and I look like hell. My teeth feel dirty and my mind is evil. I want an escape, but you can't escape from yourself."

When I went for my next blood test, it was not a pleasant experience. I was so cold that they found it incredibly difficult to get blood from my veins but continued trying despite saying how much it was hurting. Another punishment. My arm went red and from ice cold to boiling hot and then back to ice. The pins and needles started and I went into complete panic. This was not because of the blood test but because I had a flashback. A flashback is not a memory, you are taken back to that exact moment and re-live the experience with all its emotion. I was back at that ski trip when I had the panic attack that sent me into Hypoxia where the first thing I felt was pins and needles in my arms and hands.

I convinced myself that this happened to remind me of my life before "Rex" controlled my mind and how horrible it was being bullied. The reason "Rex" was now in my life and was my only friend. This all caused me to have a huge breakdown when I returned to the clinic. Two staff members helped calm me down and just held me tight, reiterating how much they cared here. However, it was snack time and I was petrified that the food was fuelling the torture in my mind, that I would have another flashback, and so the difficulty in eating was taken to another level. The same staff members sat with me for an hour to help me through it, if I did not do that snack, this fear would only escalate.

As you will always find within these units and illness, there were a couple of unhelpful patients. New patients coming and going instilled fear into us, not knowing what personality would come through the door and who we would live with 24/7 within an already tense environment. This illness is demonic and possesses us, even the nicest of people can become nasty.

With eating disorders, there is a big element of comparing ourselves against each other, who was the thinnest and who was the most ill, I could never understand this aspect of the illness. But I now see it as who was the golden student to anorexia, like a child wanting to be the teachers favourite and get the highest grades. I found one patient in particular very difficult, but I turned it in my mind and tried to use this to learn how to cope with this trigger when out in the big wide world.

I was now dealing with the fear of flashbacks, the competitive aspect with other patients, beginning to struggle with body image as I was feeling unbelievably full on the intensive full portion diet and very home sick away from my family.

I came close to a complete mental breakdown.

But…

*"Throw what you like at me b****, I WILL NOT BACK DOWN."*

I began to draw to try and help. My Irish Grandma was an artist, so I felt a close connection to her while doing this and it gave me the permission to do something enjoyable and sedentary. (Though I had to get up every twenty minutes to find a way to do a form of exercise…)

But for the very first time I got immersed in something where sometimes, for a small moment, I did not hear the voices or feel the fear. The euphoria of this was amazing! But I then felt guilty for feeling good and happy. I was not allowed.

As I say, you can never win.

I then began to find it hard to tell anyone when I felt ok. I was not deserving of this. It was not too difficult to hide this feeling or a smile though, as it was very rare.

I was struggling a lot on the full portions, there was a lot of food to be eaten! It is then a vicious journey because as you gain weight you become more alert and able to feel the emotions more intensely, be more aware of feelings and the demons in your head become louder. I began to have more energy, but this meant doing more secret exercise as well as refusing food, running away, hiding and beginning to be more of an "uncooperative" patient. This was not something I had been before and was not intentional. I hated it. In fact, it added to the torment as my nature is to please people and whenever I refused food or went against rules, I was convinced the staff hated me and would no longer support me. I guess this is how "Rex" would have liked it to be. But when I pushed through and ate what was causing me such distress or did not do exercise, the overwhelming sensations and feelings were horrific.

Luckily the caring staff know it is not you and they continue to be by your side. They said to me that they need to fight my corner for me for a while as "Rex" was too strong and was winning.

I was also beginning to see myself as fat again and becoming obsessed with checking my legs and stomach throughout the day, making me want to curl up in a ball and cry at the disgust each time. I began to believe that it could not be real life, because it was such an unbelievable level of pain. I wrote in my diary, *"I REALLY don't know how to go on, I want to end it."*

Yet the next day I began with such determination again with writing, *"I need to show everyone what strength really is. I may be all consumed, but I can still shock them and be one of the most determined and strongest patients they have ever had. I will not float through as a revolving door patient. They want and like working with me, someone different, KEEP IT THAT WAY!"*

Even in such a state of distress and dealing with so much, I always wrote with such determination in between. Though so deep into the illness, I found Rachael every time. "Rex" was in control of my mind, but I managed to find a way to stay in the fight.

This rollercoaster was exhausting, to live and even to remember.

With determination, I ploughed through the food with my head down, I went into a robotic state to get through each minute of the day, it felt like the only way. Until the distress then began to come out in another way.

In supervision after a tough meal, there was a staff member from an agency with me. They come in place of regular staff when they were away or unwell. I stood staring out the window with what I can only imagine as an eerie, demon look on my face as I dug my nails into my arm and scratched up and down, unable to stop. She asked me to stop, I continued. She begged me to stop, I continued. It began to bleed. I did not react, barely blinking. She had to run and get another member of staff who had to physically snap me out of the trance and pull my hand away with force.

I remember being in that trance, being aware but completely taken over and not able to stop. That poor woman from the agency. I was now so fearful to eat and keep fighting, in fear of these compulsions coming back or becoming worse like everything else had.

But I kept on finding a way to keep myself positive and to keep going. I thought of people going through cancer and chemotherapy. It makes them feel worse to begin with, but they have to continue with it and eventually will begin to feel better. If they miss a treatment, the cancer will get stronger.

I was also in contact with a close friend from school who was battling Cystic Fibrosis. She was on IV drips, medication, oxygen and had so much more to deal with. If she could stay strong through that, I could. We messaged each other a lot through this time to keep each other going.

My roommate at the clinic also became a good friend, she saw how hard I was trying and the battle I was having so she bought me a mug with a butterfly on it to do my cup of tea challenges and invite her to have one with me whenever I felt I could. We got each other through a lot during hard times and I also helped her through difficult days. I remember coaching her out of the bathtub where she refused to move for hours and stopping her from running away when she was packing her suitcase.

And back to "Rex" in control and feeling unable to cope. *"I would rather feel controlled and starved than cope with the intensity of my mind at the moment. No amount of motivation, aims or goals are enough to help."*

***

It was my first big review with my main consultant which we had monthly. It was the time where we would discuss if we were able to move to the next stages or be granted any freedom. Whatever was agreed in that meeting was life for the next month, it was like going to court for your sentence. I was grateful that I was at least made to feel a part of the discussion here and not as though they had complete power over me. They did, but they humoured me at least. He said he had heard I was really struggling but also how hard I was trying and to take it as a reality check of how unwell I still was as I was in doubt again. To help me, they granted me access to the back garden but only to sit right outside the door, at least the fresh air and being the other side of the four walls would help somewhat. They also allowed me to come off supervision after evening snack so that I could go straight to bed as opposed to being in the lounge for half an hour watched by staff. There were staff overnight sitting on the landing outside the rooms anyway. I had to be on an hour supervision after meals and half an hour after snacks as the mentality immediately after eating was erratic with it "waking" the demons and making them angry.

This all felt like huge steps from my review and I was incredibly grateful. I finally was not being punished for struggling.

It seems unbelievable to me now that these were luxuries and freedom... Then comes my mind with its negative argument to the positive review. After the kindness and help they showed, I suddenly felt more trapped as I knew in my mind I had no choice but to do everything asked of me to continue with my allowances and show gratitude.

At the end of that day a staff member said she had expected me in tears and having tantrums through the day but was pleasantly surprised and shocked to see I was actually looking bright and managing to battle through. Another member of staff said, "that's the Rachael we know and love!"

Now I was scared to go straight to bed, scared to sleep as what if the good feeling disappeared in the night and I woke up feeling in a desperate state of anxiety again? Please do not let that happen.

It did happen. I was still finding the patient who was not complying extremely hard to deal with. Walking away from the table and not eating without trying in the slightest, exercising a lot and running away. It was upsetting many patients as she was being granted freedom as well. As I say, it is an incredibly competitive illness especially when living with one another and so desperate for freedom yourself.

Seeing someone walk out of the front door feeling calm after not eating while you are in complete turmoil stuck inside was not easy. But I stepped up and hugged the other patient in distress at the table and said, "we will do this together, we will recover."

After taking the lead to help us all through that meal, it was the day of a group called "out and about" where a trip was planned for patients with staff to do activities such as shopping, bowling, the cinema or museums. However, I was not able to go out and join this yet due to my physical condition and low BMI, I was the only one along with an elderly patient who was on bed rest upstairs. So now I had to watch all the patients go to the museum for the afternoon and sit in the quiet house with one member of staff. Though this sounds peaceful, it was quite the opposite! I put up a huge fight and was shouting at how unfair it was. Though I see now that their priority was to keep me safe and it was the right thing to do.

It is as though there is a part of you that is an unwelcome stranger, a multiple personality where the person you do not like comes through involuntarily. Causing a scene with such anger is not in my nature but it happened constantly.

At one dinner we had fishcakes on the menu, and I felt at ease with this, but when it was served with a white bread roll, I did not react well. I had already eaten two slices of toast for breakfast so it was going against a big rule of mine to not be allowed the same food twice in a day. We also had sandwiches in the evening, so there was no way I could deal with the repercussions of my mind if I were to have the bread roll. But I still did not want to let the staff or other patients down, the ones I had recently shown so much strength to and who had showed me great support.

What do I do?

I ate incredibly slowly with debating in my mind how to get out of this situation. I wanted the other patients to finish and leave so that they did not see me refuse it. I felt trapped and I was reacting like I was trying to figure out how to get out of being a hostage. At the time it was similar.

When the patients had left, the member of staff tried so hard to make me eat it, but I picked it up, looked at her in the eye with intensity as I squashed it and ripped it, got up and threw it into the bin with such force and anger in my body language and expression. This sounds dramatic, but I described it as an "out of body experience". I could see myself but was not in control, I could see what I was doing but could not stop it, I was fully taken over. When I went into the lounge, it was as though "Rachael" returned, "Rex" had done its job and I was left to crumble to the floor and cry. How could I possibly defeat that power? Now left to panic that the staff would be angry and that I would be left alone to deal with "Rex" for life by myself.

I was refusing food more often, and the secret exercise was increasing. I was becoming the patient that made it hard work and staff found hard to contain. It was not me.

I wrote in my diary that, *"Refusing food makes me feel almost as bad as eating it, but it does not make me feel like I don't want to live"*.

There was a new atmosphere and dynamic with a change in the group of patients. Many were not complying, it was becoming like a game and forgetting it was a hospital where we were fighting a deadly illness. It was the downside to it being a lovely house, with less of a prison-like feel and no punishments for not following the plan. If the illness was strong, it would play.

I tried to keep focused on my journey but was getting very claustrophobic in the house and in my head. I began to think that it was a trap, they had lured me in to thinking it was a place to help and support me, but actually they were here to torture me. I had to escape. The game just went to the next level.

The juice was poison. It was not because of the calories and the sugar that I stopped me from drinking it but because my head convinced me it had been poisoned. It was why I was feeling so drained and tired, it is why my mind was hallucinating. I recognised that a sign of being taken over by the illness was when I started to go dizzy and lightheaded, and that began to happen.

The member of staff with me had to become incredibly firm and made me write down what was happening as I could not speak. I could not show her the letter yet, she said to show her later when I was back in control.

At my next review, I was confident that as my weight had been going up, despite the secret exercise, that they would give me a little freedom. I was asking for one walk at the weekend and to do my own washing, to which the answers were no and that I would not be allowed for another few weeks.

I did not feel underweight, I was not as underweight as the other patients who were allowed to go out all the time. Why were they doing this to me? But the members of staff said I was. That my mind was over-powering and I had lost all concept of what the truth was.

I went out to the garden to process it all and to calm down, I was laying on my front with my head in my hands when I was shouted at to come back inside because I was swinging my legs and had been told I was not allowed to do that. It was apparently exercise and calories I could not afford to burn at my supposedly low weight. If only they knew just how much exercise I was managing to do secretively throughout the day. I actually dreaded it, knowing how much I now had to fit in each day. When the staff said I seemed better and seemed as though I was coping more, I felt so guilty at the fact I knew it was because I had managed to do 100 squats in the toilet or sit ups next to my bed. I was in too deep, I could not cope without it and so they COULD NOT find out!

I was caught.

I was in the downstairs toilet when a very experienced member of staff had a feeling I was up to something and this time followed me and therefore saw the shadows of me jumping. Knocking on the door she asked to speak to me. The feeling at that moment is hard to explain, complete and utter fear. I did not know what to do, I could not cope even with the exercise, there was no chance without it. They were going to be so angry with me. I had to try and get myself out of it.

I opened the door and cried. I tried to desperately convince her that I was just moving my legs while on the toilet and would not want to counteract all my hard work. In the state I was in, she chose to tell me she believed me. I felt humiliated at the desperation and the shame of how pathetic my cover story was, like a child. Obviously she knew I was lying, that did not take a detective, but she also must have seen how serious it really was. Though of course I knew that it would be handed over in the staff meeting.

"I'm screaming out in agony. I can't do this. Not the way they want it, by sitting around doing nothing but eating all day. I'm filled with terror at how much "Rex" is going to be pounding at me for getting caught exercising. I can't manage. I need a new way to cope. Dehydration? Run away? Burn myself with straighteners? Silence myself?"

Still somehow, that tiny glimmer of strength came through and I thought that I now HAD to stop the exercise I was hating so much and was able to surrender. At least I was trying to hold on to hope.

"I so desperately desire to live a normal life. WHY did it get to this point? I can't take the thought of the journey ahead. Seeing the patients at the later stages still struggle with being controlled, having to manage cooking, menu planning, life challenges and it just being another stage after discharge to just desperately try to stop a relapse. It is too much. Too exhausting. I just want to be and live like everyone else. But I can't. Anorexia is in my head. Anorexia is controlling me."

After five days where we had a lot of the agency staff in and many groups cancelled, another mind game commenced. It began with the same question, "Am I meant to get better?" As it was the first week, I was not meant to be able to do exercise because staff were watching me closely, yet now all those members of staff were away, so no-one was really stopping me or there to support me if I were to stop myself from exercising on my own accord, going against the demons. Adding to this, I became convinced that I had made it all up, everything. That this was actually just my home and it was in my imagination that it was a hospital. I was not unwell at all and did not have to sit and eat all day, I had made it up and came to believe it was true so that I did not have to do anything with my life, just be lazy and selfish. But I could not snap out of it, could not wake up from this nightmare no matter how much I tried.

It was making me incredibly stressed and anxious, I had to get out. I ran out the door and out the main gates to take a walk/run around the block. I felt an enormous sense of relief! When I got back, no-one had noticed at all, no-one said anything, which confirmed it was all in my imagination.

My head was all over the place, not knowing what reality was any more.

I had my next monthly review with the main consultant. I had to make sure I had written down everything I wanted to say and make sure to fight my corner as much as I could to be allowed more freedom or to have my care plan adapted.

I did not stand much chance having been in so much distress but fought my corner of needing the freedom as it was feeling so trapped and within my mind 24/7 that had caused this. And I was given something! Yes! I could... put my washing in the washing machine. I could not go take it out and hang it to dry as well, that was too much for me. I was not allowed on any walks at all, or on the "out and about" trip in the week, to do yoga or even to go upstairs for half an hour in the day. Another month like this. How? How is it humanly possible?

I went into the garden to try and calm myself down and to find my strength, but I could not this time. Then the main nurse came out to tell me off for swinging my legs again. It had now actually been put into my care plan that I was not to do this.

It was the worst timing, so my response was an outburst of shouting*** OFF! *Just tie me down why don't you?! I'll just become a vegetable, or is breathing too much exercise as well?"*

They had clamped down on my every movement. Swinging my legs, moving too vigorously on the swinging seat, going into the kitchen to get a drink too much. I even still had to ask for someone to get my pyjamas in the evening and change downstairs with staff supervision after two months of being admitted.

I had to run away.

Another patient who was allowed out came with me. We said if we were caught that we would say she saw me about to run and came to get me, so that she did not get into trouble. We went around the block chatting in the free world and it felt amazing. When I got back, they had not noticed again. This was great! Well, for my mind it was, as it was a new activity to run around the block at any opportunity in the day.

I would sit in the front garden against a tree reading so the staff would see me there all peaceful before they went into the kitchen at the back of the house to prepare a meal or snack. I had been watching to see how much time they usually took to do this and learnt how far I could go and run with enough time to sit back down by the tree, catch my breath, and be called in to eat.

The stones out the main gates were too loud, so I had a pathway from the tree through to a gap in the bushes to jump through. This led to a bus stop and many times people were there, seeing this girl jump out of nowhere and run. I wonder what they must have thought!

The first time I did this, I felt incredibly weak and dizzy afterwards and I was taken by surprise just how little energy I had. I did not put it down to being physically unwell but blamed them for keeping me as a vegetable and used it to now think I had to get my fitness up to stay strong.

Just once a day was enough, it kept the voices quiet. But then it became twice. Then before each meal. Then in conjunction with exercises in the garden behind the shed. It was relentless. I could not manage this anymore. I had to fully admit to the staff how bad it really was. I needed them to help me stop, to stop "Rex".

I knew the illness would try and stop me telling them once in the meeting, so I wrote it down in a letter. At the end of my review, I still had not read it. It was like when you try to jump into cold water and keep saying to yourself "now", but don't quite go! Until that extra bit of courage makes you step and then you cannot turn back… so I quickly manage to say, *"no I have to tell you something!"*

I was too daunted to have all the senior team there, so my consultant left the room so that I was with the nurse and occupational therapist who I knew well and saw on a daily basis. I began crying uncontrollably and shaking, saying I was terrified. The nurse sat next to me and put her arm around me telling me it is ok, that it was safe to tell them what I needed to. The staff there were unbelievable in their level of support.

I could not talk through the tears and fear so passed the letter to the nurse to read aloud. It was as though I was pleading guilty in a courtroom and about to be sentenced.

They were so nice about it all and were not angry with me. They said they had realised I had been fidgeting and walking wherever I could, but then I really began opening up and told them how that was nothing compared to what I was doing from morning to night.

I had not shown much emotion for a while or cried, but now I could not stop. It was a huge release for me, finally the secret was out and they could now help me through it.

I was now seen as mentally unstable and to be monitored closely, I was no longer allowed access to my room in the evening or any walks for a while until it came from a healthy place in my mind. They also put me on an anti-psychotic medication, this helped me finally sleep through the night as well for the first time in many years.

In my follow up session with the occupational therapist, I had to go through the exercises and routines I was doing through the day. I felt so ashamed and felt "Rex" pleading with me not to do it, but there was no going back now, I had to tell it all. She was quite shocked how much I was able to get away with, but this illness was incredibly deceptive.

It felt a relief to not have to do it anymore, I had my first peaceful shower without adding exercise and it felt… good!

It did not last for long and I went out for a walk. Now being monitored more closely, they phoned me straight away and a member of staff came to find me. I now felt in slight panic that I could not do this anymore. No escaping.

The staff admired me owning up to it all and were respecting how hard it was after seeing my distress and I could not let them down. If I could not yet do it for me, do it for them. They knew how much I wanted my life back!

"I just went in the garden, ran on the spot, paced around and then did a few push ups and squats. Do I feel better? Not even slightly. Why do I do it? F*** sake!"

The next morning, I used all my strength to not do my exercise as soon as I woke up or in the shower. I was exhausted from the mental energy it took to fight against it, it felt like a full days' work. At 7:50am I gave in and did exercise.

After my mid-morning snack, I was desperate to go out for a walk. The urge, the need, the drive was overwhelming. I went to find a member of staff who was helping with my exercise addiction in the hope she would understand and let me go… now that was delusional! When she said no, I made a run for it, but the head nurse was also called and they managed to catch me and with arms of both care and restraint, took me back inside to the lounge which they had to vacate of the other patients to lock the door and contain me. I was shaking and crying while screaming that they had to let me go, it was inhuman, it was torturing me. They stayed with me for as long as it took to calm me down and explained to me that I had to completely stop everything, or it would always be an unhealthy relationship and have a grip on me. They said if a serious alcoholic or drug addict had "just one hit" a day, would that be acceptable and allow them to recover? Or would it become out of control again fairly rapidly?

That afternoon I then had to watch the other patients leave to go play laser quest, the agony of it all was unbelievable.

Knowing how much the staff were there to support me and how much they would help me was the lifeline. I was still trying my absolute best to refrain from exercise, and though giving in to it at times, I was not doing anywhere near as much. Now I had convinced myself to do it every other day and only toning exercises so that I could build muscle and not just gain the weight in fat.

Of course this was another trick from "Rex", and other exercises slipped in regularly. It then became alternating toning days with cardio days. I started to get up earlier, knowing when the staff were in handover from the night to day shift and went for a run around the block.

What on earth was I meant to do to stop this?! Evidently I wanted to as I would not have admitted it to staff or found them for help when the urges were too much. I was even being watched a lot more with very little freedom. Looking back now, I do not know how I managed so much still! "Rex", you are powerful. Scarily powerful.

But, fighting back, I decided to create a games day for everyone on the Sunday, which was a difficult day with no groups or distractions. I made a "Staff VS Patients" poster to put at the breakfast table with the order of games we would play such as cards, very mini table tennis and board games with music on in the background all day. It was the first time in so long that my personality came through, the first time I heard myself laugh as well as everyone else. I had the slight voice in my head telling me I should not be happy, but I managed to ignore it and have FUN! I remember it incredibly well as we all pulled together through the day and it felt so good to have given that gift to myself and everyone else too.

It was a revelation for me as I managed the day really well. It was a day where the food menu would have normally been particularly challenging for me with an ice cream at 10:30am after a big breakfast and having bread at every meal. I had refused things on this day of the menu several times, but I would not let it ruin the fun today and it showed me that when I am out living a real life, food would not matter so much or dictate how I felt.

We also took a group photo and when I saw it, I was taken aback at how thin my wrist was, that my face was not as healthy as I thought and that I looked quite pale. Next to the four healthy members of staff, I could see I was still not well.

One of my friends came back to visit and I was so nervous just thinking I would be judged on my appearance, forgetting it is not what my friends out in the real world are like. I came up with many ideas for entertainment as I was worried it would be awkward. How ridiculous, this was my best friend for years! And the anxiety, as always, was not necessary as we sat in the garden chatting and laughing for hours. The only unfortunate thing, and I remember very well, was when I had to go in for snack and the snacks were incredibly challenging with "Rex" then telling me I had been lazy just sitting in the garden today. I chose a chocolate bar, shaking and sweating while opening it like I was diffusing a bomb! I then left it and ran away. The member of staff followed me and got me into the lounge where she gave a brilliant motivational talk, but "Rex" was better. I was not doing it. When I returned to the garden, she said I came back with a different personality. It was "Rex" now.

I had my next review with my main consultant and Dad came up to join, Mum had to work, and I was glad she was able to do so now I was being cared for.

The morning of review, I had to have my hair dried and straightened by staff on the landing because I could not be trusted. I am not sure what I meant by this, if I was seen to be at risk of burning myself with the appliances in the state I was currently in?

I was petrified as admitting to the exercise addiction would be raised and I thought my Dad would be so ashamed of me. When I was first caught exercising and denied it with the pathetic cover story, I had called Dad in tears about how I had been accused of this. When I now told him the truth, he did say he was angry and frustrated, but at the illness and shocked at how I had managed to do so much.

The review went well, though I was still given absolutely no freedom. My BMI had to be at 14.5 but was still just under 14, which I found incredibly hard to believe. My consultant said how strong my illness was and could see it was tormenting me, but that I seemed a lot calmer and mentally more stable. If this continued over the next month, then I would be able to start the "Out and About" weekly group and go on one walk a week.

The biggest motivation was that my next review was on Mum's birthday and if I complied and worked hard, they would let me stay overnight at a hotel with them! They also recognised how much tennis and going to Wimbledon meant to myself and my family so would grant one day leave to be able to go with them in 6 weeks.

After my review I was allowed to go out with Dad for the afternoon as the journey was so long to visit the clinic. We went into the city to buy a pair of jeans as it had been my dream to be able to wear jeans as they had not fitted for a while, but now leggings were causing such body image problems. fantastic. I remember those jeans so well and doing a twirl in them on Skype to show Mum. Though looking back now, I looked so tiny in them, they were still very baggy at a UK size 4.

We then went to the pub, some things never change! And I was given permission to have an ice-cold diet soda and even to go down the slide and on the swing. I was 21 years old! However I cannot say this has changed much either, only I'm able to give myself permission now and to have a little care-free fun as opposed to a way to exercise!

The prisoner stage to my admission had a glimmer of hope in ending, I felt positive and my personality was beginning to come through. It was going to be an incredibly slow process with a lot of fighting to do, but I would go into the next stage with my armour well and truly on!

8

The Continuing Fight as an Inpatient

I had the most dangerous addiction, an addiction that had become a lethal drug to me but was usually promoted for good health. Every squat, every push up and every secret run that I did was giving "Rex" strength and slowly killing me. We are constantly told of the dangers associated with substances such as heroin, cocaine and alcohol, but when was it ever said that exercise or even just a walk was potentially lethal? How was I supposed to go against something that is all over the media and said by medical experts as something you *should* do, as well as by the demons in my mind?

I went to find a member of staff when the pressure in my head was building into what I recognised would become an explosion to my own detriment. I wanted to run, but I felt like this time I would not be able to stop. It was a scary feeling. When I was explaining this to the member of staff, she asked me to stop swinging my leg which I was doing in the most minimal and natural way, and that pushed me over the edge, I shoved her out of the way and fled. My fears were confirmed when I could not stop and as the staff knew I had gone, I had no reason to make it back in time before they noticed. When I told myself to walk, "Rex" said run. When I told myself to go back, "Rex" said keep going. The staff were calling me, I would not answer. It was really cold and it started to rain, my hands and feet were burning and I was now anxious as to what the staff were going to say, so I listened to the messages and to my utter relief, they were caring and not angry, so I finally managed to go back.

I realised I was scared of recovery. I had lived with "Rex" and in a clinical environment for so long, I was used to my bony, tired body and my whole day being about the illness. I do not remember life without it, can I live without it? But I still was not going to be giving up!

I continued to do my best with the strength I had left, but I kept getting beaten down and each time it was worse. I had a lunch of cheese and potato cakes which looked so horrifically greasy, I felt an immediate sense of shock and fear. I sat anyway and began to eat. I got through one of them, but when it came to the second one, I left the table to "go to the toilet". I just wanted a bit of space to breath and intended to go back in, but when I turned to step back into the dining room, I got the most terrifying sensation of what I described as being *"internally whacked"*. I remember this well, I can see myself crumble to the floor in what I can only imagine as looking incredibly dramatic, though I wish I had been acting. I was sweating, shaking and crying on my knees with my head in my hands struggling to breathe. I was again taken back to that panic attack on the ski trip when they had to talk to me like I was a young child and coach me to do the simplest act of standing up, walking to the sofa and sit with the staff with the focus being on just breathing.

Despite this reaction, somehow, they got me back into the table to rise above this and beat "Rex"! I sat down, picked up my fork... then threw it across the room and ran. I went straight upstairs and into bed under my duvet where I refused to move. *"I can't do this, I'm not strong enough."*

That evening at dinner everything was wrong.

"The wraps are huge", "There is more juice in my glass", "This are too many carbs".

Every bite of the wrap felt like torment, there was no way I would drink the juice and eat the cereal bar, so after my fruit I left the table. A member of staff came to get me, I was quite close to her being a similar age with similar personalities and in other circumstances, I am sure we would have been good friends. She had also suffered severely with an Eating Disorder and recovered which gave me hope. After two hours, she actually got me back to the table, when I sat down and froze, she took my hands and made me look her in the eye to say, *"You CAN do this, you HAVE to do this, it is the only way to weaken it."*

And it was the sincerity, the look in her eyes that I knew she meant it and she feared I was in dangerous territory of losing the whole war soon. So in response I said, *"I HAVE to"* and with no further thought, I downed the glass of juice and shoved the cereal bar into my mouth. I felt both horrendous and good! She literally picked me up and spun me around, hugging me with such pride. A moment I also remember very well.

The exercise was getting worse, even more than before I admitted to it. An incredibly powerful illness to have been able to manage it all while being monitored more closely. Whenever I was on my own for a second, in blind corners I knew, in the laundry room, *anywhere I could!* I was refusing food each day, my mood was erratic, and I overheard two members of staff talking about how concerned they were by the strength of my illness and that they had to do something. I was also so distressed by how desperate I was to be at home with friends and family living a normal life but knowing that I would not manage a single day.

Somehow in my next review, I was given a walk on the weekend to the park and allowed to go on the "Out and About" weekly group! It may have been in the attempt to help how almost delusional I had become. I was so happy, until "Rex" reminded me that it must mean my BMI was now at fourteen. This sent me into a whirlwind of emotion, I cannot even tell you why, I do not know myself. I have never understood this as I did not have a desire to look so thin. With the anxiety this was now causing me, they agreed to tell me when I hit each BMI mark of fifteen, sixteen, seventeen and finally eighteen as my head was playing nasty games with me by not knowing.

But the running away and refusing food continued. The head nurse tried to help at one point and she is a very strong character who showed "tough love". When she saw there was no means of getting through to me, the staff looked at each other as if to say, "we told you" and at a complete loss. It broke my heart to see, I wanted my fighting-self back and to make them proud, but I could not find it.

The next day I managed the whole meal plan and did not give in to exercise. YES, she is still there, I found her! I also had a therapy session where we began to make connections to how I felt which was reassuring.

I recalled when I was once lured to my old junior school for a school fete as a "reunion" with people who were my friends and not the bullies. When I went, I had been set up by these people who were now friends with the bullies, and they attacked me. They kicked me and punched me onto the floor while hurling abuse at me. It was years after leaving that school and I have no idea why they did this as I had not spoken to them since leaving. My parents said perhaps they saw on social media that I was doing well in my new school and in life, so they were jealous of that. I ran home crying with a black eye and bleeding. We explored the problems I have with body image and that it was not "looking fat" I did not like but feeling heavy and weighed down as opposed to light and airy when I was at a low weight. I even hated when I needed the toilet and had to go straight away to get it out of me.

I also refused to let myself be seen as weak. I would not even let myself cry at my Grandma's funeral. I remember my ears and throat burning and my head throbbing from wanting to burst into a waterfall of tears and heartache but was adamant and did not shed a tear.

However, as progress was being made with my physical health, I was given more freedom. It was now summer and so they had put the swing ball and table tennis out in the garden and other summer games which I was now able to play.

A lot of patients were physically well and capable to play these. It was a place for an all-round recovery and so these were positive incentives and managing real-life. Though for me, it became just another way for "Rex".

I spent endless amounts of time standing there hitting the ball as hard as I could round, and around, and around on the swing ball, standing with an umbrella in the other hand when it was raining. Then continuing to play table tennis and games with the other patients at any time they were there, even when I felt so weak and tired, the drive to keep going was strong. It was what the other patients were doing, and the positive summer feeling showed us all so happy, I think even the staff purely saw this and not what was going on in my mind which was just shouting "more, more, more".

With "Rex" being fuelled, my mind became more demonic.

"I don't like the person I am becoming. I feel angry and snappy at people, in particular the staff."

This played into my mind as another reason I am supposed to be hidden away with anorexia. "Rex" told me this was my true personality and it was ugly.

When my evening milk looked a different colour, I shouted, *"it is f***ing disgusting for f*** sake."* And when I got what I thought was a larger snack size to the other patients, I shouted, *"you gave that to me on purpose, well f*** you."* It continued with so many small things, when I was told to do or told not to do any simple task, I felt targeted and quickly retaliated. When they tried to help me and give me reassurance, I reacted fiercely saying that they did not understand so do not bother trying to tell me I can do it.

When other patients tried to be friendly and say they struggled with similar things to me or if they were good at something I was good at, I would snap. I had the sense of them stealing my identity. Those who know me now and knew me before I had anorexia will know how out of character this is for me. I love working with people, often quoting, "teamwork is dream work" and want to be nice to every person that comes my way, proud of every success. Anorexia turned me into someone completely different and unrecognisable both physically and mentally.

However, there were two new patients that I did start to get on well with, Sarah and Alice. One of our first encounters together was when they covered for me while I ran to the shop to get them sweets. I got to run, and they got forbidden sweets, everyone was a winner! They were like true friends, not "institutional friends". It felt like I was hanging out with the girls in a normal setting, chatting and laughing which diffused my current turmoil a lot. I have so many memories of us all together.

I felt torn and at a horrible middle point in recovery. I had my personality back and some normality with Sarah and Alice, as well as having gained weight out of my previously critical condition, but I was still struggling so intensely mentally. I felt as though I now had to make a choice as to whether I fully let go of "Rex", just manage the illness for life, or to stop fighting and give in to "Rex"? It was maybe the reason for my anger, I felt lost and unsure as to who I was anymore, which path was my destiny.

***

At my next review I was suddenly given so much more freedom and responsibility, I was given three walks a week in addition to doing weekly yoga and going on the "out and about" trip. I was also beginning two breakfast preparations a week, where I got to make my own breakfast supervised by staff. I was going to start "snack out" where I would challenge myself with a member of staff to eat a snack out at a place outside of the clinic once a week. I no longer needed weekly blood tests and would have these just as requested.

I should have been so happy with this progress, but of course it was never as easy as that. I was scared, I was no longer needing to be monitored so intensely with being a lot healthier, and no longer had the ammunition of the statistics of being unwell against "Rex". I had to start learning how to live life independently and how to fight "Rex" in these times of freedom.

Yet when I asked about my weight targets, I was told my BMI had not reached fifteen. I was not even at the weight I was admitted at last time, but I felt huge and disgusting. I had such a long way to go physically and so much more fighting to do mentally. I did not want to gain any more weight, I could no longer see I was underweight and so eating was even harder. I now had the intense body image problems of before, in addition to the much deeper and darker issues. HOW was this going to be possible?

Another event that should have been full of joy was my parents and sister coming to visit. I had not seen my sister since being admitted or my parents for a few weeks, so I was terrified of the physical difference they would notice. It was not vanity and just wanting to look thin, it held so much importance to which I cannot explain. It was how people knew the demons were strong in your mind and when you gain weight, the demons get stronger, but people see you as being *better*. What if everyone then left me alone with "Rex"? How would they know the torment I was facing as I was not always allowed to say it aloud? There was also a sense of shame, that I did not deserve to be well and had also failed, I had failed to obey the master in my mind.

The fear of my family visiting was unnecessary.

"I had the best afternoon with Mum, Dad and Amanda!" When we were all together outside of the clinic, the fears became a distant memory and when Amanda said to me, *"Your smile is more real, not forced and covering up the pain, I can see my little sister coming back",* it made those fears even more redundant and reminded me of why I was doing this. Amanda is not always the best at talking about her feelings and emotions, particularly back at this time, so when in family therapy she opened up, I was really taken aback to hear she feared for my life each day and just did not know who I was any more. It hurt, but it was good to hear the truth from someone I knew would only say something like that if she honestly felt it and not to "make me get better".

She also told me she had expected me to have gained more weight, that I had a long way to go and promised she would be honest with me on this and tell me when she thinks I look healthy. That meant a lot to me as I held complete faith and trust in her.

Though the week should have been positive with the visit from my family and the progress from my review, it seemed to have gone from bad to worse.

We had a replacement chef and the meals were awful which did not help and when the meals also came out looking different from what we knew, it felt impossible. I was refusing meals and this also caused me stress in how it would be seen by the staff and impact my progress, so when it came to the third meal in a row I wanted to refuse, I felt trapped. We had soup and a roll which I had come to quite like so had not expected a problem. The rolls were homemade, wholemeal and really fresh, so quite enjoyable! So when presented with huge white rolls that did not look so appetising, the war of "Rex" vs. Rachael commenced inside my head. The member of staff supported me in the battle and together we won against "Rex" to eat the roll while uncontrollably sobbing, but that was not going to be the end of it, and I became possessed once more.

It was dark and raining outside and I stood up, took my socks off and ventured outside to walk up and down the sharp stones. I was to be punished and feel physical pain to take away from the mental pain.

It must have been a frightening sight as I stared blankly, clearly not in control of my own body, like another scene from a horror movie.

***

I continued to find everything very tough, I felt extremely low and was struggling to cope with the feeling I was just falling deeper into the dark hole. When I went for one of my supervised walks, it was with an agency staff member who was the same age as me at the time, 21. It felt so demeaning that she was studying and training to supervise me and then going out with her friends for the evening while I tortured myself because I had eaten a bread roll.

When we returned, the founder of the clinic was there with her son who was the inspiration behind opening the clinic when he recovered in a similar setting in Canada. She introduced me as the girl who did so well last time and told him of my travels to Ghana and France with such pride. She acknowledged all of my achievements and not the fact I had relapsed and was back in hospital. It gave me such a boost and I told her I was going to do even better this time!

It allowed me to get myself back on track with a surge of positivity and by the time review came around again, I was given a little bit more freedom of being allowed in my room three times a week for half an hour and to have more days of preparing my own meals with staff.

I was also beginning cognitive therapy now that my BMI had reached fifteen and therefore could process more in this way.

I could see why this was necessary. In the first session, I was asked to think back to when I was bullied in junior school at 8 years old, but I could not remember in much detail and so I called my Mum to help me. She explained how one day I came home from school with a sudden obsession with my legs being fat, especially after a photo was taken of me in my leotard at dance school. I said to my Mum *"I wish I could cut my legs off."* She suspected that one of the bullies had called me fat to have started this from what seemed like out of nowhere. It was my legs that were always the biggest issue for me with my body image which shows how powerful the mind really is to have relayed this information throughout my life, for it to have stayed within my subconscious.

However directly after this, I interestingly turned to comfort eating and used to eat dinner at my friends' house, not tell my parents and eat dinner at home afterwards as well. I also had to be cut back on how many cakes and biscuits I was eating at the after-school club I attended.

Working through these events helped to cope a little more when starting to answer the question, "why?".

The visits from family were becoming less anxiety provoking. My Dad and Kim, my other sister, came to visit and we had a really fun day shopping, getting my hair cut, going for a coffee and playing in the park.

Amanda came again too, we went into the city and had "tea for two" and began speaking more on therapy and what I had been exploring. She told me about a time she thought I had died on the sofa. She was looking after me at my parents' house and when she came to wake me in the morning, I was not in my bed. She ran downstairs to find me curled on the sofa, but I would not wake up. She thought the worst but she was fairly calm, not because she did not care, but because it had been on all of their minds that it could happen any day and it was more that the day had come. However eventually I woke up but I had severe conjunctivitis and was very unwell so I could not open my eyes. Amanda had to ring my parents because she was extremely concerned about whether my body was able to fight off an infection.

She went on to say how she did not care what I physically looked like, she just wanted to recognise me as her little sister again. I cannot believe what my family and friends had to go through, what they had to see and experience.

After visits, I become more and more homesick and desperate to leave, but I realise how much I still struggle with the meals and exercise, knowing I am not even close to managing at home. A staff member used an analogy of going on holiday.

"You get so excited thinking of the destination, but all the packing, planning, airport and flights are exhausting, you just want to get there! You know there's no other way but to endure it and when you finally arrive, you forget the journey and relish the destination."

I was getting through the journey. I was now allowed on a walk a day and was no longer on any supervision after meals and snacks. The biggest achievement was being allowed out for a meal with my parents on my Mum's birthday AND to stay overnight at the hotel with them. It felt like such a great responsibility and I was both nervous and excited. My mini holiday destination after the journey!

I remember this night very well. We went to a restaurant that I had to go to with staff the week before to *practice* the meal I would have, so that I could relax on the night. When we went back to the hotel my parents wanted a drink at the bar and when my Mum ordered

a Brandy, I got a sudden surge of courage and asked if she would help me to have one as well. It felt amazing, I remember feeling so free and happy, saying cheers to my parents and smiling with them over a long-awaited drink. When we went back to the room, Mum gave me a shoulder massage which was an even bigger step for me as she could barely stand to look at my frail frame before and I would not let anyone see my shoulders or touch me. We both felt at ease, laughing at my pampering from Mum. What a memory.

Returning to the clinic after this and being faced with the current horrible atmosphere, I used the new found strength and motivation to try and manage. It had become so competitive with no-one wanting to start their meal first, developing more eating behaviours to be worse than the one next to them, talking about how they have managed to lose weight and so on.

When I had my first day where I prepared all my meals with staff, the other patients kept telling me what to choose for the lowest calorie option and not to choose to have a bread roll or cheese. So I thoroughly enjoyed making my cheese and pickle roll and sitting at the table with such a smile, engaging in normal conversation with the staff, enjoying my meal and then walking away with a calm and confident demeanour once finished.

I quote, *"Get me out of this s*** hole, "Rex" has got the wrong person. I don't belong here, this is not my life."*

My positivity and motivation continued with a member of staff that does not usually take the patients for snack out but had requested to come with me. We ordered lattes and it felt like two friends out chatting about life. She said how shocked she was when I arrived to be admitted to the clinic looking so skeletal and gaunt, she barely recognised me and had to walk into the office to compose herself. I had gotten to know the staff so well in the last admission and formed such a bond in this special place, but I did not realise how much it had affected them to see me back like that.

Following this snack, we went bowling for the "out and about" group. Everyone was so miserable so I stepped up to make it fun, challenging people to see what different way they could bowl etc. Then a member of staff got a handful of skittles from the machine and jokingly offered them around, of course everyone refused... except for me! I took a couple and the shock on the patients faces but pride from the staff member was amazing. At this time, this was a huge challenge and a big step.

My friend who had visited a few times came again and she noticed such a difference in my personality compared to the last time and we were allowed to go out as well. I had remembered how much the afternoon snack ruined the last time she visited, so I lied to staff and said I was having snack out with her and lied to my friend to say I had snack after lunch at the clinic. I was doing better but it was not a miracle. *"I'm fat enough now to be able to miss one snack"*.

We went to play crazy golf in the park and had so much fun. She then *"allowed"* me to have a diet soda and a lollipop while sitting on the grass in the sunshine. It was a moment that I felt I could remember what it was like to be free, happy and belonged with my friends.

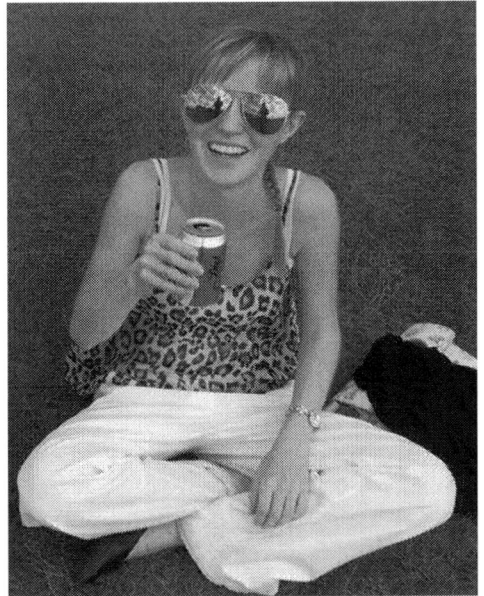

Things still were not ideal. The drive to exercise was still incredibly excessive and when people came to visit, I based what we did on how much walking, standing and moving we could do. When my friend had to leave, I walked all the way back to the park and around it again, taking forty minutes to get there the long way and an hour to walk around it, then back to the clinic – the long way. My feet hurt so much that I had to get the foot spa out so they did not notice how red and puffy they were.

I was also still refusing food at times and now that I was on full "meal preparation days" where I prepared breakfast, lunch and dinner, I was sneaky in always managing to cut back by weighing slightly less food out or quickly throwing something away if I managed to distract the staff member who was supervising me.

Yet my personality was coming back and I was a lot calmer. I do not know if this was because of the exercise and cutting back on food, or a sign of recovery. But in the next review, due to my change in persona and also nearly at a BMI of 16, I was allowed free afternoons on Wednesdays, to go into the city at the weekend and into my room once a day. This all being used to the advantage of "Rex" and not for my own enjoyment.

I used one of my free afternoons to try and buy new clothes, all size 8. When I returned to the clinic, I decided to try my jeans on that I brought with me as an aim to fit in to. When I was admitted they literally fell straight down. The second time I tried them, the waist fitted better and they stayed up, though very baggy. This time, they fitted. But I was told I was not yet at a BMI 16. They are lying to me. I do not need to gain more weight, that is now proven. I rang Mum in panic and she tried to calm me down by saying recovery is for my mind not my body, and that is why I needed to continue. She also rationalised that a BMI of 16 to 18 is actually only a small amount of weight on each part of my body, but it was not going to be so easy to move past, it had fuelled the fire of "Rex".

Looking around me, my roommate was hysterically crying and screaming each night while packing her suitcase and saying she was escaping. Another patient was on "arms reach supervision", where a member of staff had to follow you 24/7, so was always shouting at them to leave her alone. Another was always running away and self-harming, so police were being called constantly. I was struggling within my mind and therefore quiet, there was not time for support. But in a first aid course, you are told to go to the quiet casualty first, they are most at risk with urgent need of help and that the screaming casualty was at least alive.

I was also beginning to have more independence and freedom, I was not ready. I had my first free afternoon to go out on my own and I tried with all my will power to get the bus into the city, but I walked there. It took nearly an hour, I told myself that I would get the bus back, but when it came to it, I walked. Now this was set as to what I would have to do every time. I was never happy doing it, constantly arguing with myself with every step that I should not be and worried someone would see me, tell staff, and then I would have this free afternoon taken away from me.

However when I was there, I did challenge myself to try clothes on and though I felt the overwhelming hatred of myself looking in the mirror, I found a way to find a form of acceptance to the way I saw myself. I also took a huge challenge on to have a bra fitting, this meant being exposed to someone else, allowing them to touch me and to be uncovered from my baggy clothes. Not only that, but it was a big issue for me when I was growing up and having to wear a bra was one of the indications, so when I first needed to start wearing them in school, I did not want my parents to know because it meant I was not their little girl anymore. I would pull away from hugging them so they could not feel the straps.

To further add to the challenge, I treated myself to a new bra in my new size, thus accepting my new figure as well as spending money on myself.

So the afternoon had positive achievements too.

I was hiding behind my new freedom and too scared to have it taken from me after being under such intense supervision in one room for so long. So when I was seen both physically better as well as enjoying my freedom, it became a lot easier to get away with things again and for "Rex" to start gaining power back.

After a very challenging breakfast, I felt mentally traumatised again with the amount of fat and sugar that was in it. Even to this day with a healthy mind-set, it was a lot! So I do not blame myself for finding this so hard. But I coped by instantly signing out to run around the block, then walk around it again and then did leg exercises in the toilet when I got back. No-one noticed.

After the breakfast so full of sugar, I could not do snack so refused this by saying I had a bad stomach. The nurse gave me paracetamol and Gaviscon and I found that I became panicked by these having calories too and swallowing them told my mind it was a snack.

I found lunch just as hard with the amount of fatty meat and oil in it, but yet again I ate it quietly while looking so calm. Meanwhile, my mind was very loud and it was hell within. To help cope I signed out and went running around the block, but this time there was not a drop in anxiety, it was not enough to get rid of all that horrible stuff I had just put into my body. I felt invaded and trapped with it inside me. I contemplated being sick as an option but knew I could never do that, and luckily never did.

"I'm fed up and angry that food can so drastically ruin my day and make me feel so horrendous. I just want the day to end again, but I don't want to have to keep wishing my life away because of a meal. I just want to be okay."

I believed that everyone thought I was greedy, fat and disgusting. I felt distressed feeling my legs wobble as I walked and was convinced that I could not see my feet over my bulging stomach.

I had told myself I had to stop the secret exercise when I was allowed a walk a day, but I had not. How could I when I was becoming this fat WITH the exercise?

My sister came to visit and surprised me with two friends of ours as well. We went to Great Yarmouth and had so much fun around the beach, playing crazy golf and in the arcades, it felt good to be laughing. They were easy people to be around and I felt relaxed with them not judging me, so for a while I forgot I was a patient. It was a saviour with giving me the boost I needed to stop what was becoming a spiral into a dark place. At least postpone it slightly.

I had been too scared to voice my concerns as I had a home leave planned in a few weekends time to go to Wimbledon and I did not want that taken away from me. So that day arrived, and I was leaving the clinic on a Thursday evening to return on Sunday. It was a huge step after four months as an inpatient with just a few hours on my own recently, so I was nervous.

After such a long time and being far from home, the few days of leave should have been exciting and about seeing everyone again, especially going to Wimbledon which is a special day. Instead, all I wrote about was the food. I cannot tell you who I met or what I did, how Wimbledon was or who I saw play. I can tell you I screamed at my sister when she wanted me to have cream with my strawberries, that I would not have the picnic and had to bring my own, that I cut out many ingredients at dinner times but managed to achieve eating a jam doughnut with my sisters.

So much quality time missed, so many memories that weekend should have had, but it was robbed from me through fear of food and being angry at anyone I met for saying I looked well. I interpreted this as having gained a lot of weight and that I looked fat. I also think that the anger I felt with this comment came from desperately wishing they knew how unwell I still was in my mind.

When I returned to the clinic, my illness had been fuelled by being "free" over the weekend and from being sneaky in managing to cut out many things from my meal preparation when staff turned their backs, while also doing hundreds of sit-ups, planks, squats and walking. I wanted to do my cross-stitch, to draw or to watch Wimbledon, but I just could not allow myself. Unfortunately I was actually noticed to be brighter and with a more vibrant personality, the fear and anxiety was supressed deep within me, so when I was asking for support spaces, the staff did not see it as urgent and the time never came with all the distractions from the screaming patients. I felt like something was brewing inside me, like a duck with its' legs going so fast underneath the surface but looking so relaxed above and gliding smoothly along the water.

With the way I was feeling and how much I struggled with home leave, I did not think my review would go very well. However, as I had been hiding that so well, I was given a lot of praise and freedom. Of course I was happy with this, or "Rex" was. I was now allowed what was called "free access" so no secret walks, I could sign out whenever I wanted to. I was also allowed to prepare my breakfast without staff supervision, they obviously had never noticed the cutbacks I had made. I was to eat on the independent table so without staff supervision, though it was next to the table with the staff present. The biggest step was that I could go home every other weekend. This proved to be difficult for me, even with managing the travelling as it took four hours on the train so I would have to make sure I kept moving as much as I could as opposed to sit down and relax on the journey.

I was not ready for any of this, but this is what happens when you deceive and do not say when you are not ok.

***

I was in a difficult position as when I was admitted, most of the other patients were much further into recovery so I was on my own at the beginning stage. They had now left the clinic and I was on my own at the latter stage, with all new patients who required a lot of the staffs time. My body image suffered to a worse extent with being surrounded by the new admissions and the pain this caused me intensified. I would get changed four, five, maybe six times in the morning and reduced to tears with every outfit.

I had the voice in my head calling me a fat, greedy s*** and I felt like I did not belong there. Mentally the illness was still very strong, it was so deep that no-one saw it. Dangerous. Very dangerous. I was using my freedom to be constantly walking and my feet hurt so much. I had said that when I was allowed one walk a day, I would stop the secret exercise and cope with everything better, but that had not happened and the demand just increased. It was never enough.

I walked into the city again on the weekend. This time I was hit by the biggest sense of loneliness I had yet experienced as it was a Lord Mayor Procession with music and entertainment throughout the streets. I was watching all the families and groups of friends enjoying the festivities, smiling and dancing while I sat in a coffee shop looking out the window in turmoil over ordering a latte. I realised just how much I was missing out on in life and consumed with the horrible sense of distance between me, my friends and my family, both physically and in soul.

Seeing the silver lining in every situation, both then and to this day, I managed to see the connection between my emotions and my anorexia as I found the rest of the day so difficult with body image, feeling disgusting about myself and finding the food incredibly hard. It carried on into the next day where I had a tantrum at breakfast and ended up going on 6 walks that day with it haunting me… the reason was because the toast was not toasted enough. I refused snack and I could not sit down and watch the Wimbledon final without going upstairs every time the players changed ends, to do exercise.

It was all heightened after how lonely and upset I felt in the city. "Rex" was my way to cope but was also the reason for it. It was my only friend, but my worst enemy which reminded me of the bully in school.

Even with all the secret activity and not following my meal plan, I was told my BMI was nearly at 17 and they were pleased with my progress so I could begin playing sport. The struggles in my mind were still so well hidden and I was physically out of the danger zone, so I was allowed to play Tennis on the weekends when I went home and to go and play Badminton every week with Alice, the patient that had become a true friend.

I relished being able to play sport but knew it was all signs that I was on my last stage to be leaving the clinic, and that frightened me.

I continued the running, the walking and the exercises in my room. I continued making the cutbacks when I prepared my own food, I refused food and walked away from the table. But none of it was making me feel more able to cope or lessen my anxiety. It used to help to an extent but now I was at a loss of how to cope. I spoke to my parents and to staff, but nothing was making the pain go away.

"I've cut down on the exercise, it is not helping anyway, so I only went on my short run around the block before breakfast, the walk around the block after snack, shopping in the afternoon and an hour walk before dinner. I feel so lazy."

I was signing out before and after every meal and snack to walk. The walks becoming longer, having to walk faster to get the distance in before the next group and therefore never getting any support. I could not sit down for a second longer than I needed to, I could not *ask* to sit with staff to talk!

The body image specialist took me clothes shopping to buy new outfits. She made me feel good and excited to begin having a normal body and wear normal clothes. However it was difficult that the tiny sizes did not fit any more, but the size 8 clothes were still loose. I hated my body as it was but had more to gain.

I wore one of my new outfits on the train home on my weekend leave and I was struggling with eating again with travelling being so sedentary. I was about to get up to walk up and down the train when a group of Irish boys began talking to me. I engaged in conversation and before I knew it I was laughing with them, real laughter that felt so good and I realised they would have no idea that I was on home leave from a hospital clinic. They just spoke to a girl who looked approachable, not ill. THAT'S reality.

That reality continued through the weekend when I was able to play tennis again with Dad. A sport that was a big part of my life from a young age and still is to this day. I ate a good lunch before and grabbed a banana for more energy, I felt normal!

I became upset when I did not play well and angry at the illness for taking this from me, but overall it was amazing. That evening was my sister, Kim's, birthday and we all went over for a barbecue. For once I could join in with burgers and then we played children's games, it felt like the old days again. It made me think that though I may not have liked my body, it allowed me to live a life like this.

Returning to the clinic was harder this time with the weekend being so normal and enjoyable. However I had not been doing the full meal plan, especially at breakfast as the portion size was unreasonable for anyone. The staff realised I had been doing half portions on my meal prep days as well so put me back on supervised breakfast preparation and another patient told them about the exercises in my room.

In review I had been desperately asking to do half portion breakfast, or what would be normal portions in society! Of course they would not allow it as it is always assumed to be from an anorexic point of view, though everyone at home had agreed with me. And again of course I was also now being stopped from the room exercise again.

So, I made a deal with them that they would now tell me my weight on weigh days so that I could see exactly what stopping the exercise would do, or not do, as opposed to driving myself insane with analysing myself every minute and thinking that I had gained 10kg (22lb) from missing a walk.

It was helpful that we had a group trip to the beach at the weekend, but to cope with the journey, I went for a walk before and did 200 sit ups, I was still somehow managing to defy the monitoring from staff with my exercise. At the beach I built a sandcastle, went for a walk and played bat and ball with a smile so that staff would think I was just relaxed and happy, when all I wanted was to move and exercise. I missed out on photos with my two friends enjoying that beach, something I live to deeply regret.

That day was also the tennis club championship at home which I had participated in from a young age, and my sister was in the final. It used to be known as myself and the opponent she was playing against each other every year. I felt angry, sad and frustrated, but also jealous and even replaced.

The next day I met Sophie, an incredible friend whom I have known since childhood. She moved away when we were 6 years old but somehow we still knew how close we were in life and stayed connected. We did not see each other for 10 years but would write letters and phone each other all the time. When we finally met again in person, it was as if we had never been apart.

She had moved to Ipswich so now being in hospital in Norwich, we were closer and we met for the day. It felt so normal, shopping and chatting all day, but again I had an element of these mixed emotions. She was studying at university, had a house, a job, a boyfriend, a life. I had "Rex" living in a hospital.

Everything was building inside me with seeing everything that I was missing out on and all I wished for, but yet still felt I could not reach or have. I was feeling such rage and anger and yet I kept my calm exterior, until I ran to my room and screamed into my pillow, smashed glasses against the walls and started tearing at my hair, before calmly returning to the lounge. Suppressing this sort of emotion could not be sustainable.

***

I had another review and with this, more freedom. I was now allowed to go swimming when I convinced them it would be for body image. An element of this was true as wearing a swimming costume terrified me and I bought a tummy control one, but really, it was a good form of exercise. It was with staff support at first and though I had to pretend to engage in conversation, I was counting the lengths and each time I went I tried to get that extra one in. One day I was told swimming had been cancelled and there was no way I could cope with that, so I went on my own and started doing this regularly. It soon became having to reach 60 lengths with such fear of what would happen if I did not manage. I would dread going as I knew how long it would take and how much I hated it.

It was not making life any easier. Everything I was doing was adding fuel to the fire of "Rex" and I was missing many meals, running away, unable to have that cup of tea again and not managing the snacks I was supposed to be having out on my own. I was going into multiple shops each time and analysing every nutrition label, before walking out with nothing.

My body image was worse than ever, but on my free afternoon I decided to try on swimming costumes in an attempt to fight back again, a huge mistake. The sight of myself in the mirror was so mortifying and the intensity of the feelings made life almost not worth living.

Yet the weekly home leaves were seen to go so well. I was happy and enjoyed time with friends and family, but I walked and walked and walked, played tennis, cleaned my car, went swimming and shopping, anything I could do to be moving all the time. I restricted my food at every meal and was sneaky throughout, just like before. For instance, "driving to town", I parked at the top of the road and then walked, weighed out all my food, throwing some of it away.

I constantly compared myself to Mum and I was jealous that she had a gap between her thighs when I could just feel my horrible thighs rubbing together.

I would see playing with my godchildren in the play areas as exercise. I love it too, and genuinely this had some true enjoyment attached and freedom as they were too young to know I was so poorly and treated me like a normal, fun person. But I was seen by them as "so fun" because "Rex" would not let me stop running, jumping, climbing. I feel ashamed of this now.

My consultant still saw things as going well, so I had a planned discharge in one months' time. I could see "Rex" rubbing its grimy hands together ready for me.

The turmoil just got worse, but my calm exterior remained. In the city I was going into the arcades on my own to play on the dance machines and basketball machine for more exercise. I was unable to choose a lunch, buying several and throwing them away as if someone took over my body, an involuntary impulse driven by "Rex".

It was a 24/7 argument in my mind, that I never seemed to win.

***

On the next train to go home for the weekend, I found myself looking up how much of my medication I would need to take to overdose. They gave a set amount of medication on home leave, so I only had three days' worth, I wondered if it would be enough. The reason that stopped me was that I did not think I had enough tablets, and if it was not enough, I read one of the side effects was gaining weight. However, I was now feeling paranoid that they had tricked me by putting me on this as a way to gain weight quicker. This paranoia increased when a letter arrived from Farnham Hospital, who were to be my "outpatient home team" and where I was a day patient. My weight was written down on it and said to be 47.7kg (105lb), BMI 17.2. But if calculated, that weight made my BMI 19! I was in turmoil with not knowing which was right, but by the looking at myself in the mirror I assumed the higher BMI was correct, which would then mean the clinic had been lying to me.

It made the whole weekend at home very difficult. I restricted my food and though it was raining, I dragged my dog out as an excuse to be able to go for a walk. We went to see my sister in her flat in London which was an hour drive so I had to do as much exercise in my room beforehand as I could. Despite all the efforts, I still felt fat, lazy and just far from ok.

When travelling back to the clinic, the trains were cancelled and delayed which meant it took six hours, on six different trains to get back. At the stations when waiting for the train, I was walking around and around, up and down the stairs and carrying my suitcase, which did have wheels, over my shoulder as a weight. I bought lunch to have on the train but every time I got it out, I panicked and put it away, I thought people were judging me for being greedy.

The week back at the clinic, the only thing I wrote in my diary was that they confirmed that it was my BMI that was correct and not my weight from the letter I had received. Instead of relief, it sent me further into the depression with how badly I reacted when I thought I weighed a bit more. It was the first week in years that I did not write in my diary, the first time since becoming unwell.

The next weekend that I had home leave, I was supposed to have banana cake for a snack beforehand. Sharon, my key worker, tried to convince me to have it by telling me that the staff were worried they were losing me and that I was going down a slippery slope. I still did not have it.

The manager of the clinic then found out I had been walking all the way to the train station each weekend with my suitcase for home leaves, which took an hour, so they booked me a taxi. This caused fear and panic, so I went for an hour walk before the taxi came instead.

I hated every minute of home leave again. I began having a fear of eating in front of people alongside everything else. I had to watch my sister and friend play a tennis match and it went on for three sets which made my anxiety so high in that they were doing so much exercise and I was not doing anything, but I made myself stand up the whole time to watch it.

"Today has been the hardest day of all. My anxiety sky high, no appetite and feeling so indescribably unable to cope in my mind. It was unmanageable, I did not know how to get rid of this. Getting through the day in desperation, trying to keep going, having to keep active. I actually just want my life to end".

I went for a pub lunch with my parents and I told them I was struggling to just know what to eat but that it was not even from the fear of food anymore, I just felt numb, I just felt nothing. They realised I was now suffering from depression with the enduring and never-ending fight of anorexia.

I was given a "depression score test" when I returned to the clinic and my score indicated severe depression, so I was put on more medication. I argued in my mind if I had made up the answers to get these tablets, I had Rachael vs. "Rex" again. Rachael said, "I know every answer was truthful", "Rex" said "I wanted to be given more tablets".

***

My discharge date was in 10 days and in my last weekend home before that discharge, it was the same food restriction and extreme exercise regime, I kept thinking how this was going to be my life every single day with no-one to stop it again very soon.

When I had the sense of complete inability to cope, I had choices enter my mind of drinking myself into oblivion, starving myself or taking all my medication. These thoughts, these "choices" were becoming worryingly regular, and I wanted to ring the clinic to tell them, but I could not. I did not want to be discharged yet, but "Rex" did.

I had not reached the BMI I did last time when I relapsed. I left confident and happy last time, when I relapsed, this time I was in constant turmoil at every minute still. I was terrified.

The quotes direct from my diary are all I need to tell this next part of the story.

*"I'm still being controlled by the b**** and to be honest, I'm not willing to live like that, but I can't get rid of it, so what does that leave me?"*

*"I can't carry on life rationalising and calming myself every time I eat. Comparing myself to everyone, wondering if they are going to eat or why they are not eating. Feeling compelled to walk and walk, do more and more. Arguing if and what I should eat and how much I can move at every point in the day. I'M F***ING FED UP!"*

During my last week at the clinic, I had such an attitude on me that I did not know I had when I was arguing with staff over everything. When a member of staff tried to stop me storming out, I shoved her out the way. As I was a week from discharge and care planned for free access, they could not stop me.

I just walked and walked until I did return for lunch.

But lunch was wrong too. It was not the right portion, it looked completely different. A patient I was friends with agreed and we both got up and walked out of the clinic in unison, feeling a little like naughty school girls and giggling at this. We went to get sushi and sat enjoying that, until the head nurse called us. She was quite a strong person who you did not want to make angry, and we really made her angry! I felt ashamed and disappointed, a part of my personality was to not upset people or be seen badly, but I was not doing so well with that.

I had a review that day and was worried what would be said or taken away from me. But nothing was said at all, despite admitting that I was really struggling, and evidently the day showed that, but they just kept saying that I will be fine. When I said I was going to screw up, they simply told me that I would not.

I had shown my struggle, I had voiced my struggle. Back to square one feeling like no-one was helping, no-one was hearing me, why would you not listen?

"I searched how much paracetamol was an overdose because I did not think I wanted to die yet. I just want someone to help me."

Then I went to the shop.

When I had taken them, quite thankfully I realised I was not ready to die yet and became worried. I went to find someone straight away though could not get the words out with feeling so ashamed. When I finally did, they called an ambulance and I was taken to the emergency room where I had to wait two hours for blood tests so that they could see the damage. In this time I called my parents. I heard their voice and just cried. Though they were used to this, they knew something was different, something was really wrong, and they waited patiently for me to tell them. They were really caring but quite shocked with not realising how bad it was in my mind. At home I did seem ok, it was not their fault, they were not to know.

The results came back at 1am, the doctor told me it was a close call but I would be alright. If I had taken one or two more tablets, I would have had to be admitted and put on intravenous drips.

When I woke at the clinic the next morning, I was a mess. Agonisingly tired and agonisingly destroyed. The tears flooded through me and just collapsing onto staff. So many emotions from fear of what "Rex" could do to me, to wishing I had taken those extra tablets.

The staff were so supportive, now that I had *shown* the despair I was in. Though I had tried to explain before, I cannot blame them for not realising the truth when I had put on a fake smile and seemed as though I was doing fine with normal fears before a discharge date. The head nurse, who was so angry the day before when I walked out of lunch, brought her new puppy in for me, but I could not smile, could no longer even fake a smile. I was broken.

Though every meal that day was torture, through tears and walking to and from the table, I managed. I was still fighting.

My consultant was called in and he asked me to seriously consider staying until Christmas. Three months more. Missing university again, turning down my job at Go Ape again, letting my friends and family down again.

"I don't even know what to write any more. I just feel so low and still have horrible thoughts in my head that I wish I had taken those extra tablets. I do not feel like there is anything stopping me from doing it again properly, or something else. I know I need to talk to someone about how I feel but I cannot bring myself to do it. I feel like such an idiot for thinking this way."

Every diary entry following was about how much I could not live with the fear, anxiety and dread of every waking minute, which was also at night as I could not' sleep.

I was still allowed on my walks, but my bag was searched every time I entered the clinic. On one of my walks I thought, *"I really would not mind it if a bus hit me right now."* And then I started having to refrain from jumping into the road on my walks.

I was scared of my own mind. I had to stay. I thought I could possibly stay for just a few extra weeks and not months and that way I could still go to university, but I knew that would be a halfway measure with no committing to either decision. I was not safe, so I knew my only option.

At the time I felt so weak for failing, but now I see how much strength I had in making that decision. Thank goodness that somewhere deep down, I still wanted to fight back.

Until the nightmare began once more. I was back to square one with being on all meal and snack supervision, allowed only 1 walk a day with staff, eating on the supervised table at meals, not having any meals out and only able to use the stairs once a day.

I had worked hard for 7 months to gain freedom and on the date that was originally my discharge date, I was taken right back to the start. I fought every single day against the frustrating level of supervision and lack of any personal space. When I was admitted and had all of these restrictions, I was incredibly unwell physically and therefore without any energy, whereas now I was near a healthy BMI and on these restrictions, it was a nightmare.

9

Back to Square One as an Inpatient

I managed to hold on to positivity and hope. I had a tiny sense of relief that I now could not do all my illness driven walks or maintain the illness in any way. I can draw again, do my cross-stitch, read and play games. It was not my choice so it was safe and I could not feel guilty for it.

"Today is the first day on all of my restriction and it has been absolute torture. But do you know what? I survived, I managed."

Another day without them, I may not have been saying the same.

I had been going to play Badminton with Alice each week which had been such a saviour as we allowed ourselves to have fun and not let it be ruined by our illnesses and exercise driven. We also would play table tennis in the garden at such leisure, mainly just chatting, and not power table tennis!

So when I went to get ready for badminton and was told I was no longer allowed this either, I flipped. I was not physically unwell anymore and they knew how much this helped. I could not see why I was not allowed with another patient, a social activity. They were adamant and had control over me again so just had the biggest tantrum, screaming at them from the stairs and refusing to eat my snack. It looked like it was because I could not exercise so would have set me back in being allowed to go again, but it was the mental torture to stay in the lounge all afternoon with no groups and nothing to do.

Alice and I had become such good friends and despite the setting we were in, we were constantly laughing. That afternoon she stayed in with me, even though she could have gone out. She was my saving grace throughout this admission and even in this hard time, she stuck by me. Whether a chat or dancing around the lounge, she always managed to make me smile and lighten up the situation. We would play hide and seek, remembering vividly when she hid in the tumble dryer and I hid in the smallest gap between the cupboard and ceiling. We were there for ages realising we had both hidden, therefore no-one was looking! Except staff of course when we had gone *"missing"*. My key worker, Sharon, found us and even she laughed at how we managed to get into those spaces. Alice giggled, *"don't play hide and seek with anorexics"*.

We also played pranks constantly, mainly on my key worker, Sharon, as she had such a good sense of humour. We hid in a cupboard jumping out to frighten her with the best reactions every time, she was addicted to drinking tea, with two or three cups on the go at once, one day we hid her industrial size box of teabags and created a very long and winding trail of said teabags for her to follow and find it. She was not so happy at this one, somewhat annoyed, but we still could not stop laughing. Times like these were vital in staying in the battle against "Rex".

The next morning I woke up sweating with anxiety. Dreading another day. It was like ground-hog day, deja vu, some sort of twisted experiment, not my life. How could this be someone's actual life?

It was to be my first weekend at the clinic for a while and I was dreading it. But then I remembered how much I dreaded the days at home knowing how much walking and exercise I had to do with no one stopping me. Again there was no winning.

I tried to enjoy it as I had no choice but to stay in, so I watched a movie, played games and was allowed to go swimming with a member of staff, so that helped a lot. But watching all the patients go out to the city for their free afternoon was not easy, and I knew they all walked there too. One patient even messaged me to say she had walked all the way to the arcades, where we used to go together, and then how fast she had to walk all the way back because she was late. It was incredibly tough and unfair for her to do this, but I tried to think that I was killing the illness and would be the free one in the end.

I just wish that I had been at this stage with the group of patients who were in when I was admitted. They were not exercise driven or competitive, no-one refused meals, they sat together chatting about life, dressing nicely in their newly recovered bodies and helped each other through. The atmosphere I was now in was a lot of unwell patients both physically and mentally, with a competitive environment, constant refusing of food, shouting and hostility.

My parents were coming the next day and I was looking forward to them seeing me calm and at ease when they most likely were expecting me to be very low or erratic.

It ended up being the most relaxed time that I had with them, "Rex" had taken a hit and it became about quality time with Rachael, not the chaos of "Rex".

There had been a marked difference in my mood, though things were by no means easy and the thoughts were all there, but they were easier to manage and I was able to refrain from fully indulging in them with the fear of what may happen again if I did.

My eldest sister rang me, though of course a very caring person, she was not one to show emotion and had more of a matter-of-fact personality. So when she called me just to hear my voice and said "Love you Rach" at the end, my whole outlook shifted into what my real life was and what I was aiming for.

That did not last... the next day I titled "F*** up Friday". None of the food was *"right"* in my mind and resulted in refusal of snacks and getting up at dinner to scrape the spread out of my sandwich because it was so thick. This aggravated other patients and Alice came into the kitchen to see what I was doing, shouted at me and then stormed off too.

I had upset everyone, and though I still ate the meal, it was seen as a refusal because I took the spread out. The guilt flooded in as I may as well not have eaten it if I was in trouble and everyone hated me anyway! I ran off again and called my Dad who reminded me that I needed to do this to recover for me and not for a good report or to be a good student.

"Ultimately I am scared, I still dread each day, the drive to exercise still haunts me. It is creeping back... just by playing swing ball and swinging my legs but that is where it all started before. Why and how is it going to be any different this time? I had been feeling better, yet here we go again. And that's what finalised my decision that I do not want to live any more".

Keep going Rachael. Find a way.

I attempted to go down the route of trying to have fun! When an ex-patient I was friends with came to visit, I was allowed into the city with her and another patient, Sarah. We decided to buy roller-skates and skated back in them! I thought I would be good at it, but I was not and they had to hold my hand all the way back! With the laughter of this and concentrating on not falling over, I got an amazing sense of freedom. We then decided to stop at a pub and have a beer for a snack! A relief to have a winning day again, experiencing life and giving me a reason to try and cling on.

The following week I continued to try this tactic of fun.

Sarah and I went to the park again the next day with our suspiciously large bags which held the roller-skates. It was so much fun, we held hands going down a ramp and both fell over, for a moment we were terrified we had injured ourselves as our bones were quite fragile and now our elbows and backs hurt a lot... how would we explain that one? But when we got up we just ached a little with nothing visible, thank goodness!

When we began skating back, we saw a member of staff and a patient on their supervised walk. They had not seen us yet, so we were frantically trying to get out skates off but laughing too much and failed miserably. Luckily it was a relaxed member of staff and patient who laughed and would not tell anyone! It was like we were being caught stealing or breaking the law.

The following day we went to the city together, we were both quite driven in walking there and back but decided to make up for it by going back to the pub! However, we got kicked out... I wanted a rum and diet soda, a can of soda though so that I knew it was definitely diet. He kept trying to give me the soda from the pump which distressed me too much in case it is not right. When trying to ask him again for the can, he threw the drink away and shouted for us to get out of his pub! We were shocked but laughing so much. That is what kind of antics we should be up to and the trouble we should be in, instead of for not eating cake or for moving our legs too much.

We went to another pub, got the rum and *can* of diet soda followed by a tequila shot!

I was allowed to go home again for my birthday, which would be the first time since I had been put back on restrictions after the overdose I had taken. I felt so much calmer, it was such a relief to be able to sit down more so I could get a taxi to the station with my bag and sit on the train. At home I did not have to be so sneaky and spend all of my time going on long walks and therefore got to actually have time with my friends and family.

As it was my birthday weekend, I wanted to get my hair done but with having it styled and highlighted, it takes from two to three hours, sitting down. I debated cancelling it a few times but I managed to do it! When I got home and found myself on my own, I still did not do any exercise and waited for Amanda who was coming over to play Tennis.

In the evening, I had planned to have drinks with friends, but most of them cancelled last minute. This would have usually made me upset and would have thought it was because they did not like me, but I would not let it ruin my birthday this time, it is just life! So I arranged to go and play "Top Golf" with my sister and a couple of friends. When we arrived, it was so busy with no availability. I was now quite anxious with the second plan failing, so I asked the manager to help and told him it was my birthday and I was on weekend leave from hospital. Don't ask, don't get and nothing to be ashamed of! There were two men about to take a bay and I asked if we could join them, something I would never have had to confidence to do before and even my sister and friends were not so sure, but I made them! We had so much fun, I was confident and even a little flirty. One of them asked for my number afterwards which I gave to them. What a transformation and boost of morale!

On the day of my birthday I allowed Dad to bring me a green tea in bed, I was nervous that he would not have made it right, but I challenged myself. I then spent the day with my parents and went to the trampoline park with a friend in the afternoon. This was an exercise driven choice and it was full of kids, so I felt a little abnormal that I had chosen to do this as a 20-year-old for her birthday. Though that is a part of my natural personality too! In the evening, Dad and I cooked us all dinner at home, it was a special occasion for us to do this.

Another huge milestone was Mum taking me shopping the next day. I was very anxious as my body image was a big issue, especially comparing myself to Mum. But we had such a good girls' day and I found jeans in an adult size that fitted me well and I also felt good in! I came bounding out of the changing rooms to show Mum with pride, both our smiles speaking volumes.

The weekend was the least "illness driven" one to date and Dad was then taking me back to the clinic to join my big review. They had agreed to help me get into sport in a healthy way and also suggested staying until January. This was so I could go home for Christmas with the safety net of returning to the clinic as it was a stressful holiday for someone with an eating disorder. It would have been incredibly difficult to be discharged and thrown straight into the feast of Christmas.

The positivity continued. Another huge step was refraining from a morning walk and doing life chores instead with sorting out my university deferral and paying for my car insurance, things I had not had the pleasure to do in years and that I most hated! It gave me a sense of independence, adulthood and normality. I was excited at the prospect of getting a job one day and paying my way in life.

It continued further! We went on the "Out and About" group, one I remember very well. We were taken shopping again, but no-one had any money to spend. I suggested to Sarah and Alice to find crazy outfits for each other to have to try on! This involved telling each other our sizes and having no control over something that is quite sensitive for us all, especially myself at this time. But I held my head high and I felt proud to tell them I was a size 8. I chose the most outrageous outfit for Alice, but when she tried it on, she looked amazing! She was one of those people who could pull off anything. while next to Sarah and I who looked ridiculous. Thanks for the fluffy hat and jumper with the rainbow raincoat, leather leggings and silver stilettos Alice!

We had such a laugh!

And it stops. *"I feel like I can't cope again."*

We had social snack out, where we went out as a group of patients and staff for a snack, and I was told I could not have the oat cookie as it was too low in calories and I had always chosen the "healthier" options, so I had to go for chocolate, it was challenging but I managed with Alice's support.

Then at lunch we had one of my favourites, Salmon Tagliatelle, so I had not anticipated any difficulty. But when I saw the pool of oil and butter under the spaghetti, I freaked out. It had never been like that and I had to keep asking for reassurance, the staff were trying to convince me that the water was not drained off properly, so it split the sauce. I did not believe this for a second.

My instinct was to shout at them and run away, but I knew that made me feel just as bad, I felt trapped. I began eating, but with every mouthful the voice was getting louder. I was thinking about the oil and butter inside of me, how disgusting it was, how every mouthful was destroying my body. Out of nowhere the thought that I would take another overdose afterwards came, as if it were the only way I could get through the pain to eat the rest of the meal. It is how intense these feelings were, and it concerned me that it was a thought that was still so readily there in my mind.

Luckily I had a one-to-one session and a group straight after the lunch so I could not go out. After these, the urge had reduced and I thought of how my parents and consultant would have reacted, that it would ruin the weekend I had planned. None of the thoughts against it were for myself, my own health, or the want to live.

"No, I would not do it".

But the voice was shouting in my head saying, "go on do it, do it, do it", so loudly I felt like it would never stop, so I ran to the shop and I bought the tablets. "Rex" saying, "Yes do it, do it". I did not want to and it became a direct battle in my mind, hearing the distinction of the voices. I ran as fast as I could back to the clinic to find a member of staff to tell them before I did anything. What if the voice did not let me stop taking the tablets this time? It was a sense of possession again and as though I had no control.

The power of it. I suddenly felt it was a punishment for having fun lately and laughing, allowing myself to flirt with a boy and give him my number, for being close to a maintenance weight, and having the audacity to consider the prospect of having a real life.

"My toes are bleeding from how much walking I did today. This gives me a little buzz and made me contemplate self-harm to cope. I do not know what is going on with me, but all these crazy thoughts keep entering my mind and although they feel like silly little thoughts, that is how the overdose started too."

"I had the urge to jump into the freezing cold lake at the park, I do not know why. Either an act of self-harm to feel the pain of the cold water, or to drown."

"We had quiche at lunch, I talked to staff about my anxiety, and it was hard throughout. I just wanted to smash something and cut my hand with it."

We had another difficult lunch and I feared what might happen if I were to push through it with my current state of mind, so I set off out of the clinic and bought a light lunch instead. I then walked to the tennis club which gave me a sense of hope and excitement as I had forgotten just how much I missed it, how much I missed the social aspect of it and the sport itself, so not purely for the exercise. But then I could not stop walking. Hours and hours and hours. The staff from the clinic kept calling but I would not answer until I heard a voicemail where they said if I did not contact, they would have to take things further by sending the police to find me as I was a threat to myself. So I called to say, "I'm ok, back soon" and hung up.

When I arrived back, I was searched and questioned multiple times if I had taken anything. When did I become this person?

***

In my review I was told I had reached my goal BMI of 18, despite all the activity and cutbacks on food. I felt fearful but also ashamed and guilty. I was not sure why.

To my surprise though, I still had a good weekend at the clinic that followed this news. It was Halloween so we played games and "bobbed for apples" which was hilarious. Most would not play as the apples and even water that may be slightly consumed were extras into our diet.

Sarah and I had planned to go trick or treating dressed as clowns in our roller-skates. We painted t-shirts, bought wigs and wore colourful trousers. I do not know how we went out like that and on our roller-skates, but we had been there for a year so we knew the staff routines and could meticulously time it! It was the most amount of fun I had had in years and I remember it so well to this day. Realising how trivial the rebellion really was considering our ages, we knocked on the door of the clinic to shout "Trick or Treat" to them, and thankfully, they laughed too but were also in pure shock of how we managed it! We anticipated them confiscating the sweets, so we had stuffed some down our roller-skates. It made the other patients smile too, so was worth it all round! But the next day we got into SO much trouble from the general manager at the clinic. I had never seen her so angry or been told off so much there. I was not sorry though, it made me realise I wanted to live a normal life of a 20-year-old, not being told off for trick or treating dressed as a clown.

The following day I met my sister, Amanda, in London. We had a great day of strolling around and sight-seeing. Nothing was planned from what we would do or where we would eat, which was another great challenge for me. However it ended up being a lot of walking and little eating on my part. I felt very frustrated seeing what it was like to live without anorexic, watching Amanda freely go to different stalls and picking up a snack, enjoying a latte and a cake when she wanted it, and ordering from a menu with excitement and ease, not with fear. It is incredibly under-estimated at how life destroying it is to be so scared of food.

My friends were also all going on their yearly trip to Centre Parcs. Each year I booked to go with them and each year I ended up being too unwell when the time came. Here I was again, in hospital missing out, watching them all post on social media about it and being unable to refrain from scrolling through to see it all.

Then I freaked out at lunch and wanted to run off again. I told staff I was going and eating out, the nurse said I was sabotaging my admission and should think very carefully. If I went, there would be repercussions and I may not even be able to stay. Yet when all the patients were "acting up" before and refusing many meals, running away and more, there were never repercussions! Why do I get punished? I had worked so hard for the year and was now showing that I was struggling. The rollercoaster ride from seeing real life, to being told off for trick or treating, told off for struggling and reaching a healthy BMI, but still with a very unhealthy mind triggered the following poem:

"Do I run or do I follow?
You make me numb, you make me hollow.
When I think I'm there and can see the light,
You take control and make me think you're right.

Standing from afar,
I can see the demon you are.
But in desperation and fear,
You are the first to say, "I am here".

Without your safety, without you there,
Can I really live? Do I dare?

But then I think,
Do I really believe,
That if I shrink,
You will leave?

I know I'm worth more than this,
And I want you to go.
But no matter how hard I try,
You just keep screaming "no".

This is why,
I have no choice,
But to say goodbye,
To get rid of your voice."

I was so glad that I was meeting Sophie again that weekend, but the thought occurred to me whether it would be my last.

We had such a fun day shopping, having lunch and chatting before meeting a few other patients at the cinema. When Sophie had to go, I felt really low at again seeing how free she was with life and feeling like I could never get to that point. So Sarah and I decided that we would go for dinner and then did a mini pub crawl for a few drinks. When walking back, we got drenched by a car going through a puddle, so we ended up returning to the clinic late at night, tipsy, looking a state and giggling away! The perfect pick-me-up and what a Saturday night should have been looking like at my age!

So why I then woke up the next day in such an anxious state, I do not know. It was unpredictable.

I left the staff a note saying, "*I have got myself in a right f***ing state, I'm panicking and freaking out. I need to get out so I'm going to get breakfast and then I promise I'll be back.*"

I did go to get porridge from a cafe and felt calm afterwards, until a sudden wave of anxiety came that I should not have had it, that it was too much milk and that now I've had too much liquid so I should dehydrate myself for the next couple of days. Yes, that is how I will cope with this and rectify the mistake I have made.

I did not drink anything for 6 hours but then gave in when playing laser quest, or more pushed past this stupid punishment my head was making me do.

I was going on another home leave and I desperately wanted it to be as calm as the previous one. I no longer minded that they ordered me a taxi so that I did not walk all the way, but I wanted to stop in the city to get my lunch for the train. They told me this was not care planned and I was to get the taxi all the way to the station. There were minimal places to get lunch at the station and it was close to the city, I did not understand why it was a problem and I was not allowed. After arguing, I got the taxi to the station but then walked back to the city to get lunch and then back to the station when it began pouring with rain! I got back to the station absolutely drenched, and then I found I had left my purse in the cafe in the city! I wanted to curl up and cry. I thought that this must be my punishment for not obeying to the dehydration. I walked all the way back to get my purse and then again back to the station. The positive side was that I did not find any sense of happiness at the amount of walking or exercise, just sheer dread at the cold, wind and rain.

I began writing more poems:

"It is World War Three,
Inside my head.
You would not let me be,
You feel me with dread.

But every day,
That I keep up the fight,
And I don't obey,
Or take any of your shite,
You weaken, just a bit,
With every hit.

And my anxiety,
It just shows me,
That I've done something right,
And I might, just might,

Be beating you,
But I have not a clue,
What it will take,
To get completely rid of you,
To make you break.

You broke me,
You tore me down,
You hurt my family,
We could not smile, but only frown.

But we've stuck together,
So far made it through,
And now I know,
I don't need you!"

"You make me forget the pain,
That you put me through,
I know I must refrain,
From coming back to you.

Agonisingly cold,
Fingers and toes turning blue,
Aching bones feel old,
Want to be hidden from view.

The power of your voice,
Haunts me every day,
I felt I had no choice,
All I could do was obey.

The rules I had to follow,
Made me a prisoner within myself,
And you would not let me swallow,
Deteriorating my health.

The days became such a chore,
And sport became a way,
To just do more and more,
Make it stop I had to pray.

There were scary times,
That I did not think I'd make it,
Breathing was so difficult,
But you did not care one bit.

That's when I came to realise,
That you just want me dead.
And all you told me was just lies.
So I'm choosing life instead."

I titled the next entry, *"It is a kill this f***er of an illness day"!* I felt things brewing again and had not been telling staff that I was struggling. Each day that I made my own breakfast I was making half portions and the exercise was becoming way too much again. So I took it upon myself to make a full bowl of cereal, which was a big challenge for me, and opted to go to the cinema with everyone, where I would be sitting down for over two hours, and still have to eat a snack! I realised it was the anorexia making me think it was not ok and that I DO NOT have to obey, I DO NOT have to earn the right to relax and eat.

The day was a huge battle that I thought I won, until I suddenly dropped back into fear. Thinking what if I did not get better and after all of the pain and effort from this fighting, I just relapsed again? Because I have now thrown everything I can at "Rex", but it always throws something back at me harder. I still did not even know why I had the illness when my life outside of it could have been so happy with a future so bright. What if it was just a disease I had? Like someone with diabetes, it is just the way I was, and all of this fighting was futile.

"I feel so low
And it is on show,
Within my skin,
That I'm letting you win.

If I do something right
You'll make your grip right,
To make me feel,
A pain that is unreal.

It starts with a little,
But I then become brittle,
And you can tell I am weak,
That is what you seek.

But I don't understand why,
You want me to crumble and cry,
What have I done wrong,
To endure this for so long.

They say I am fine,
That I'm starting to shine.
But they have no idea,
Of my remaining fear.

It is World War Three,
There's no minute I'm free,
Of the sheer torment,
And when I thought you went,
You'd only evolved,
After one thing I solved,
You create something new,
To make me fear you.

Will it ever end?
Or do you intend,
To stay with me,
And never set me free?"

I was back in a very dark place, and scarily over something so small. I had a difficult day challenging myself with food and was then stopped from playing badminton as we had a "one off" group to do drumming which we all had to take part in. I was angry as I was genuinely looking forward to going out to play badminton but managed to contain myself and not use my eating disorder to show my distress. So I got on with it.

When I then had to prepare my own dinner and decided to do tacos, I had to use the new "square bottom" ones which was not a problem at first, until I finished my dinner and realised they were probably higher in calories. I sneaked to the bin to see the packet and saw it had an extra 90 calories. I panicked and did not know what to do with myself, I felt in despair, I did not know what to do to make it okay. A run would not help, refusing evening snack would not help, I felt trapped. I went for a shower, I picked up my razor and brought it to my wrist...

I started scraping it along my wrist, adding a little more pressure each time, once more and it may have been the one, but I managed to quickly snap out of it and throw my razor across the bathroom. The power. The relentless power.

I had home leave again and managed well with sporting activities like rock climbing. I then, apparently, went to see The Script in concert with my sister in London. I have no recollection of this. Another memory missed.

In my next review they thought that I had now been there TOO long. So when I was battling anorexia to such intensity that it made me take an overdose, I should have gone home? A new discharge date was set for the 14ᵗʰ January, five weeks away. The last time I had a discharge date I felt hyper and giddy with relief that I would not have to eat the high calorie diet anymore and could do what I wanted – or "Rex" could. This time I felt calm and just ready to live a life, it felt vastly different which was a good sign. Was it not?

I then had a trip out that I remember very well. Alice and I went on a "social lunch" where we went out for a challenge lunch in the city together with a member of staff. We decided to go to a Mexican restaurant and we ordered a butternut squash and chickpea chilli. I was panicking at it being double carbohydrates and the portion size, but Alice kept me calm and then came up with the idea that when the staff member went to the toilet, we would order cocktails – of course I got the "Tequila Smash". We had not laughed so much in such a long time! Especially as the staff member could not help but laugh with us when they arrived, and then actually let us have them! I was so full and felt so disgusting having a sugar loaded cocktail as well, but I pushed the feelings aside to see the fun element. I am so glad I did as it is a treasured memory.

**

I did not write for a while, but things were going smoothly in the lead up to Christmas, though I recall that I was incredibly stressed and staying up late every night to finish the handmade Christmas hampers for my family. As sweet and thoughtful as that is, I should have been stressed and staying up late revising for exams, not knitting! I was given a long home leave of 8 days for Christmas and I was extremely nervous. It started off well as I had an interview to work as an outdoors activity instructor at Go Ape and was given the job, it was such a huge incentive for when I left hospital. Though it was an active job, I was sure it was a part of my genuine personality and nature, so why was I not entitled to have this job like everyone else? And I am so glad I went for it as I made lifelong friends there who then stuck by me through the years of future battles and are still my best friends now.

Christmas 2015 was the best one in years!

It was the previous Christmas that my world fell apart, the truth and the battles were revealed and the spiral from there being too painful and too tormenting for everyone involved for words to ever describe.

I joined in this year, relaxed and happy with the food, drinks, games and laughter. It was over the mince pie the year before that triggered the meltdown into how unwell I was and so when it came around to "mince pie time" it was slightly tense, it held on to a lot of memories for me, as well as it still being a food I feared. I did not know if I could do it, and then everything would be ruined. Dad spoke to me and motivated me to get through it, afterwards I called the hospital to just relieve some anxiety and then I was absolutely fine!

On Boxing Day, the tradition was meeting the extended family for a buffet of Christmas leftovers, where for years I brought my own lunch. For the first time I joined in with this as well and it felt so liberating. Though I felt quite hungry I was incredibly cautious with counting how many of each thing I had and the quantities pre-set in my mind. I was scared if I let go completely, what if I had eaten everything like a scavenger and would not be able to stop? I was more scared of the repercussions from my mind, as they had been quite severe over things such as a different shaped taco. Who knows what would happen?

The sense of normality I experienced really altered my mind-set. When I had to return to the clinic and was woken at 7am to be weighed, then go for breakfast where there was so much drama, then just sit and wait for the next meal while all conversation was about eating disorders and asking permission to do any small task… it was not for me anymore. That was a great feeling to have.

"I've got so much going for me now,
So I have to keep it up somehow.
A new job to have a fresh new start,
With the illness, I now can part.

I feel content, happy and free,
Not living with sheer anxiety,
I can really see how much I've changed,
No longer controlled or even deranged.

When I look in the mirror, it is hard what I see,
But I'm learning to accept my new body.
There are much more important things in life,
Like having children or being a wife.

So I'm ready to move on,
To show the world that I'm strong,
I've had enough of all your s***,
And I would not be missing it, not one bit."

I spent New Year's Eve at the clinic and I reflected on my year as everyone does. Though I was not out at parties celebrating with my friends and family, I could really see how far I had come and felt proud of myself.

"I remember waking up sweating in sheer terror for the day, all the anxiety, an emotional wreck. I remember being in floods of tears over a bowl of cereal and crumbling to the floor in total distress over a potato cake. Shaking and crying in desperation to go for a walk and having to be contained by the nurses. Sneaking out through the bushes for a run around the block. Doing endless amounts of sit ups, jumping jacks and planks in hidden spots and feeling like my world was going to end when I was caught, and uncontrollably crying when I admitted to it all in my review.

I remember being so distressed that I took my shoes and socks off to go out in the pouring rain and walk up and down the stones to take the emotional pain away from eating a white bread roll. I remember running up and down the garden or spending hours hitting the swing ball on my own, back and forth, back and forth. I remember having no time for anyone because I had to do my double walk after every meal.

I remember ending up in the emergency room after taking an overdose because the pain and voice driving me was too much to bear."

***

Unfortunately, the New Year did not start well. Just after midnight my Irish Grandad passed away. Though expected to happen soon, it was devastating, and in Ireland funerals happen very quickly so I was to go the next day to meet my family there. I had two weeks left of my admission, and I felt selfish that I was worrying about the impact it would have as "Rex" does not have a heart and would pounce on anything like this, and that it did. I hated myself again, passionately hated myself. I felt selfish for worrying what *I* would wear, and what *I* would eat and how upset *I* was while I knew "Rex" was using my emotional pain to make me obey it again.

"I feel like a selfish bitch. My Grandad has just died, and I'm concerned about the food and travelling instead of playing tennis and badminton. I'm a disgrace and feel so guilty."

I fought back with wanting to make him proud. It had been so long since the whole family was in Ireland together where we would now meet to celebrate Granddad's life and give him the send-off he deserved.

But I did not cope so well in Ireland. Anorexia is very emotionally connected and with the high levels of emotion around us all, everyone was on my case about food, and I struggled at each and every moment. I just wanted people to leave me alone, the shouting voices all around me so loud and the inner voice even louder. I did my best to join in, but it never seemed to be enough and everyone wanted me to do more, to do better, to eat this and to eat that. I was not doing badly and it felt like they were using me as a distraction from the emotional pain too.

Despite this, we did have good quality time together with playing games, going to the cinema, going out for meals and everything we used to do as a family. It is something real Rachael would have enjoyed so much and relished in but all I could worry about was the inactivity, being lazy, eating too much and so on. I feel quite upset by this even now, possibly the last trip to Ireland with us all together, ruined by "Rex". I am also desperately sorry to my Grandad.

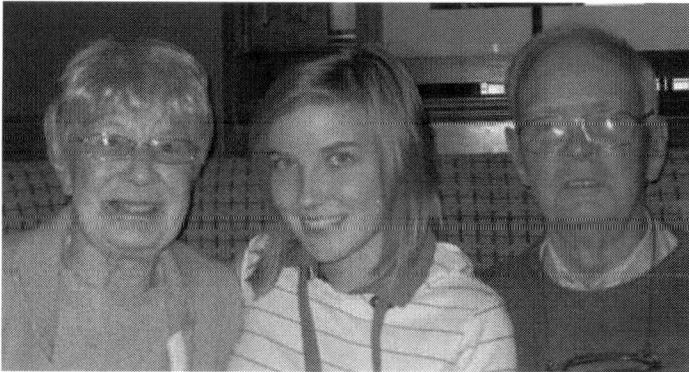

***

Arriving back at the clinic for my last week, I had my critical voice back.

"I organised games this morning which people did not really enjoy, I felt guilty and responsible. Then the second game was to guess famous people and I kept not being able to guess mine, with people groaning at me, I felt so stupid. I also always score low in the quizzes, why am I so stupid? I want to increase my general

knowledge, I should have used my time here to at least read newspapers and learn new things, but I was too busy at war.

Then I went to play tennis, but it was so windy and I did not play well, the voice in my head was telling me how useless I was in everything. I'm embarrassed at how useless I am and feel guilty being a burden to people because of it."

On my last day at the clinic, I felt so stressed, anxious and scared. I wrote, *"I fear relapse so much, the thought terrifies me."* But I remembered that you do not leave hospital recovered, just ready to continue the battles independently in the real world, it was ok to still have these struggles.

10

A Life Threatening Relapse

My first day back home after discharge was very positive. I was in a good mood saying good morning to Mum and Dad as I went to make a cup of tea and brought it back to bed. I ate well, I went rock climbing with my friend and had energy, I actually had moments in my head without any noise from "Rex". The anxiety had lessened, and I felt a sense of freedom with no upset or pull to be back at the clinic like last time. I felt like I belonged at home.

I started personal training with someone who knew about my Anorexia and alongside consent of doctors and family. I could not believe the day had finally come! I wore tight gym clothes and did not mind the reflection in the mirror, in fact, I felt very fit and healthy watching myself lift weights. I ate well to compliment my training, I was almost... normal! I was aware I was still in the "honeymoon" phase having just been discharged and when I had a vivid nightmare about relapse, I knew I had to be cautious in how much I was trying to take on, almost making up for lost time as quickly as I could and needed to slow down.

Within a few weeks, I wrote, *"No, no, no, no, no I cannot let you into my head again!"*

I was messaging people from the clinic, fatal error. I felt jealous again at them having constant support and even of the new, very unwell patients being admitted. Again, that competitive nature to the illness. I was also feeling very anxious without activity for two days and stressing about an art lesson that my friend had bought me, as it would entail sitting still for three hours. Then I also had the theatre with a friend another day, more sitting... these events should be a pleasure and something to look forward to, I should have been thankful to my friends for organising them for me.

When I started buying diet products to eat and did not attend my friends leaving party, alarm bells were ringing.

I tried reminding myself that I had just got out of a long hospital admission where I was not allowed out past 4pm and under such surveillance, I had to adjust slowly. But was that excuses?

When I had my first appointment back with my outpatients' team, where I was a day patient before, things went from bad to worse. The consultant who I did not get on with very well before was very condescending and mocking towards me. She laughed when I said I was an instructor at Go Ape and was doing personal training. During my stay at the clinic, they had helped me incorporate activity, whereas she had the ethos that I must stop everything forever. She also pointed out that my periods had not restarted so I must need to gain more weight, the worst thing was the smug smile on her face. Did she know anything about anorexia? The fact I was in a health BMI range after being so unwell at a BMI of 11 was incredible and she should have commended the hard work. I was angry in the appointment, especially when she said, *"well it is your choice not to have healthy bones and be a Mum."* I replied, or rather shouted, *"NO IT IS NOT A CHOICE, MENTAL ILLNESS IS NOT A CHOICE, ANOREXIA IS NOT A CHOICE. I'VE DONE SO WELL SO DON'T PUT ME DOWN B****!"* So I'm not sure my outpatient support was going to go that well…

I was still enjoying my new life and my new job at Go Ape, if anything it was keeping me well as I wanted to eat to have the energy for it and was making a great group of friends. We went to the pub after work, and I craved comforting warm meals that Mum made after a long day outside.

During training week, we had to learn to ascend the zip wires which was hard work! We ended up trying to tackle all five in a day, which not many do or manage, so when I did, I wanted to go for the record! I asked if anyone had included the smaller junior course zip wires to make it all 7 in a day, they had not, so I went for it! I do not know whether it was enjoying my new fitness, my natural competitive nature, or anorexia driven, but I finally had a legit achievement to be proud of and smile about! When I told my parents, I can see why they were initially just concerned, but I was angry that anorexia was the first worry and longed for it to be a distant memory, no longer a part of how people saw me.

The social occasion at Go Ape called "Cosy Cabin" was a chance to do that! This is where all the staff went to the "office cabin" for the evening to have a barbecue, drinks, watch a movie outside in the forest and then just getting incredibly drunk through the night, going for walks and playing in the play areas, it was SO much fun! And I was not even sneaking out and getting into trouble by a nurse! I then became the leader for the drinking games, I was confident within myself and joining in and then crashing on the cabin floor to sleep at 4am! It gave me such a boost after things were getting quite difficult at home again with old habits creeping in. A reminder of what *real* life was and to not end up back in a dreaded hospital.

11

How Mum Saved my Life

I stopped writing. I had written nearly every day since I was diagnosed to put the battle in my mind into words which helped me to keep fighting the thoughts. I probably could not fight any more or lost motivation to do so as another relapse began to happen.

Each time I relapsed it got worse, evolved like a disease trying to survive. The most recent relapse had me on death's door and carried into hospital, but this next one was even more frightening. Despite desperately trying to have the right support in place for when I was discharged, the aftercare failed us again. It could have made all the difference, but we will never know.

I had a job I was thoroughly enjoying, had started my university course to study sports science, was able to go out with friends and family, even had a relationship. There was no intent or desire for me to go back to "Rex", back to that dark world, so why was I going there?

It made no sense to myself or anyone around me. Doctors began to make me feel guilty as though I was doing it on purpose. Trust me when I say that no part of living that way was enjoyable. My family and friends were angrier this time as well, but not directly at me, I was angry too.

I had a letter from a couple of close friends to say that they could not watch this again, they could not watch my deterioration, ultimately watching me die. They said they were still there but had to take a step back. I could not blame them and completely understood, it was surprising they managed for as long as they did. But now "Rex" was taking the last things I had.

As I was no longer writing, I cannot remember much about this time, which shows how consumed and unwell I was. Though my parents remember it very well.

They recall the frustration that the community support system was failing us again. They felt defeated as they watched me go back to playing tennis, doing Pilates and working, while knowing the signs of an imminent relapse and from experience, knew there was nothing they could do to prevent it. They say that I declined at an even faster rate both physically and mentally, which was terrifying as they were in sudden panic to find emergency help again, as though in just a blink of an eye, I was fighting for my life again. Frail, weak and consumed by "Rex".

Though I was still cooperative to get help, I was still able to find the fight for recovery, I was willing to try new forms of therapy or be admitted to any clinic. I do remember one day quite vividly when I went for a consultation in a private clinic in London where I was told how incredible their programme was and promised a world of recovery once more, but at a great cost to my family again. The part I vividly remember was when I snapped myself out of her hypnosis that she tried to put me under without consent, to lure me into needing her help. Evidently I had a strong mind so I managed to fight it and get myself out of there! I was in disbelief, what was this nasty world? Who would do something like that? Could I trust anyone?

The deterioration continued and we could no longer wait for the "right" hospital and had to take the next available bed, wherever that may be. That is when The Priory was introduced to us. The famous Priory, the beautiful castle like building where celebrities go to get better, what an amazing opportunity. Or quite the opposite and where most of the post-traumatic stress I suffer today is from.

We had no choice, so we went through the procedures, we had to fight again for doctors to refer me, fight for funding, fight for anyone to help no longer with the energy we once had for it, but just a flat line of emotions, doing what needed to be done to go back into hospital. There still was no bed yet but it was the one that was going to come the soonest for me, so again we had to pull through each day to keep me alive until we got the phone call.

We got the phone call, a bed was available for the next week, I would be admitted on Monday so yet again I started saying goodbye to friends and family and tried to build up my mental strength to accept this was happening to me once more, then Friday evening the Priory called to tell me the bed was not available yet and I would not be admitted on Monday.

Why again on a Friday? Late in the day when there was no other help or support available? Being "specialist carers" did they not realise what this would do to us?

My parents were in a state of shock, being unable to remember this weekend just reconfirms how strong the illness was and how weak my mental and physical state had become. Mum looked up any possible clinic we could drive to, being a weekend, she knew we would not get any help over the phone, so she put me in the car and we drove around pleading for help. Only one place catered for patients with anorexia but when they looked at me, they just said my BMI was too low for them to admit me regardless as to whether they had a bed available or not.

Meanwhile my Dad was constantly on the phone calling any possible in-patient care service around the whole of the UK, they knew how desperate things were and they refused to give up, refused to accept that nothing could be done. Our resistance was weakening, but they somehow just kept going and kept me going. Finally after many calls and many visits, we found a possible bed in Scotland, but it also was not available yet. How can it be that nowhere would take me and that I was now TOO ill to be admitted? How was it fair and logical to travel to Scotland, hundreds of miles from home?

We went back to the Priory, to the head office, telling them of our desperation and they "assured" us there would be a bed very shortly.

So, we had to wait a few more weeks. With being let down and the hope of help removed, my mental state deteriorated even further, I was clinging on by my fingernails, we were all just hanging on waiting to hear when the bed would become available again. When that day finally came, we made our way there with little energy, all exhausted from the fight to make it through. My sister came this time as well to help in case anything happened to me and to be there for my parents as well. We were over halfway there when we got a phone call. It was The Priory, to tell us the bed was no longer available.

I can see all our faces to this day, feel the drop of my stomach, not wanting to believe what was happening. We cried, we shouted, we told them the desperate state I was in, I remember my Dad being on the phone to them for almost an hour, pleading for a bed in any unit there, the response was "it is not safe for her to be in another unit", his response was "she won't be safe outside the hospital". It was all to no avail and we made our way back home in utter disbelief.

He was right. But, with us all in a state of shock, no-one was thinking logically or clearly, so when I said I was going to walk to the shop to get us some bread, no one thought twice about it. Until I was gone for longer than I should have been, and my Mum suddenly realised, she realised what I was going to do, or had already done. Being a paramedic and an incredible Mum, before I knew it, I was found and in an ambulance. The paramedics said I had to drink the charcoal to neutralise the poison of the lethal overdose I had taken, or I would die. I replied with no sense of emotion, "I want to die."

We were on a time limit before it was too late to reverse the damage and though I do not remember what she said, my Mum had gotten to her knees, took my hands in hers and managed to get me to drink the charcoal. But the fight within myself and the want to die only allowed me to manage half of it, and it was not enough

I was laying in the emergency room with intravenous drips in each arm and dressed in a child's hospital gown that was too big for me, we were prepared to say goodbye as it did not look like I was going to make it.

There were times I ripped the intravenous out, I did not want them to try and save me.

I was even driven to still go into the toilets to do exercise with all the tubes in my arms.

I was there for a week and lost complete track of time as I remained in the emergency ward where it was constant 24/7 with no sense of day and night. The confusion and delirium from this and the drugs was something I can never explain.

"How am I still alive? Am I still alive? I don't even know anymore."

Until defying all odds, I came back around and was able to safely move to another ward within the hospital where they would keep me on bed rest until I was able to be transferred to The Priory.

I still did not write in my diary and I can barely remember the start of my admission. I was locked in a ward that had eight doors leading to it from the entrance of the building, requiring staff to let you through at each of them. I had no access to my room, so sat in the lounge until I was called to eat in the dining room, which was also on the ward. The kitchen was unlocked twice a day to be able to get a cup of tea or coffee, if you missed this, you had to wait until the next time. I was not allowed my phone or laptop for the first two weeks either so that I could "focus" on why I was there. Everything was confiscated; phone chargers and other leads, belts, clothes with strings, toothbrush, toothpaste and everything for the shower for risk of self-harm or suicide.

I once made a paper mache bumblebee to decorate my room and I had to make it under staff supervision in case I tried to suffocate myself with the balloon or use the glue for harm. I then was given string to hang it up for a few minutes before it was taken from me in case I tried to hang myself. It is more shocking for me to say that this was probably wise.

So I sat on the sofa staring aimlessly, if I moved around too much, I was threatened with a build-up shake supplement for doing exercise. The staff were mainly in their office and would sneakily peer through every now and again.

At certain points in the day, we would be told to go to the medication room where we would queue in the corridor, wait to go to the stable style door, put your hands out for the tablets and then have our mouth checked to show that we had swallowed them. At the beginning of my admission, I had to wait until the end before I was called as I was not allowed to stand up for that long.

The diet here was even worse than I had known in previous admissions. The desserts were huge compared to the main meal and were actually called "heavy desserts". We were also on a time limit with forty-five minutes to eat the main meal and thirty minutes to eat the dessert. If we did not complete the meal, it was calculated into build up shake as a supplement. We all sat in the lounge after the meals and those needing this supplement waited anxiously to be called in to see how much of it there was to drink. If you refused this supplement, it was added to the next day and would simply increase in quantity, you did not get away with it. If this reached the amount of 1 litre and you still refused it, you were put on tube feeding where they syringed it into your stomach.

I once reached this amount and had a huge decision to make. I sat looking at all the cups of this horrible, fortified milkshake with the image of that tube in my stomach. I finally went for the "classic Rachael" approach and picked up one of the cups, looked at the other patients debating about drinking their supplement and said, "bottoms up guys, cheers" and downed it all! I did not feel good afterwards, and I cannot go near this type of drink to this day, it makes me feel incredibly nauseous.

This was life for a couple of months I was not able to go outside because I was too unwell, and when I progressed, I was able to go outside in a wheelchair for 10 minutes being pushed around the car park.

As I finally began finding a little more freedom and independence, I began to write again, with my first diary entry being about an event that helped shift my mind-set.

"This may sound dramatic, but I had a real reality check today about what is important in life. My ceiling fell in right over my bed where I had been sleeping all night and had only just got up. What if it collapsed in the night? It would have caused me serious harm, damaged my body, stopped it from functioning. But then, what have I been doing this whole time? My poor body wants to be in prime condition to do its job and allow me to live a life, that's all. It also made me realise I don't want to die anymore because I was more shaken that I could have been under it as opposed to wishing I were."

As I could not stay in my room anymore, I had to sleep in another ward which was where the celebrities who were admitted stayed. It did not bring any excitement though as I was escorted there late at night and back out early morning so that I did not see anyone within the ward and sell the story!

The atmosphere was a lot worse here than at the clinic in Norwich. The wards for each mental illness were separate, but at times you would cross paths and I saw many sites that cannot be forgotten. The side effects of drug abuse, severe self-harm, psychosis and the torment everyone was going through from them. The alarms went off around the hospital regularly as people tried to escape, needed restraining or for urgent medical attention, though you got used to it. There was a time I will never forget when we had our time slot in the kitchen to make a cup of tea and one patient smashed a plate and started viciously slicing her wrists with it.

Patients on the eating disorder ward were a lot more chronically ill and many were sectioned, therefore did not want to get better and would make life hard for everyone purposely. One patient bought crop tops to flaunt her incredibly frail frame to make everyone feel fat (direct quote by her). She once said to me, *"you are not as far along in recovery as you think and you have an ulterior motive by supporting people"* and *"I just don't like you as a person."* Word for word without any sort of context behind it.

These were not things I could get away from, we were locked in together.

But it was not all like this. I did make a few good friends and we helped each other so much through this tough admission and I am still in contact with them to this day.

I also made friends from other wards when I was allowed to socialise with them later in my admission. I remember one time when we all watched a movie together and were making fun of each other about our "issues" which made it so light-hearted with being able to banter about it for once. Such as saying to me, "hey don't pass her the popcorn she does not eat" or "I'll share the blanket with the skinny one so I get more". All with such laughter and it was liberating after the intensity I had been living in.

When I was allowed out one evening for a special occasion, I had a few too many cocktails and when I came back slightly tipsy, or very drunk it made everyone laugh a lot. I was then breathalysed and told I could not have my medication and to go to bed, this was by a staff member I got on well with so I could not help but laugh and could tell he wanted to as well! He did however laugh when he came to wake me in the morning with an almighty hangover. I was actually pleased to finally experience one.

But overall, four months into my admission, things felt the same as all the other times. The struggles with exercise, the rules around food and I was just gaining the weight but not improving mentally. Our monthly reviews were called "ward rounds" and my consultant was very textbook about recovery and set on BMI being the only guidance to how I was doing and was adamant I must get to a BMI of 20 before she condoned me working or playing sport. My mind was strongly set to maintain at 18.5, which is in a healthy range and could manage mentally, but she would not listen to me. Nothing else was seemingly looked at, no help back into a normal life or what was happening inside my head. No-one should ever be judged by their BMI, this is a very inaccurate indication and only one symptom of Anorexia Nervosa. I gained weight very rapidly in this admission with such an excessive diet, and my mind could not cope.

I was feeling trapped again, not heard or being helped and not allowed to leave if I wanted to. I was not sectioned but if I tried to discharge myself, I would have been sectioned, so there was not much difference! I felt like they wanted me to explode and I was trying to fight against it.

"I want to smash my head against a wall, punch the wall and break my hands, run up and down the stairs until I pass out."

These wants then became real occurrences. I was becoming psychotic.

When home leave began on the weekends, it also felt the same. I had to be busy all the time and was constantly worried about the food. I was also panicking at the thought of juggling life again, with work, family, socialising and recovery. *"Can I cope, or will I just revert back?"*

I wanted to recover so much and kept striving for that lease of life. I joined in socially on the weekend to see what life could be like and sometimes would eat, drink and go to bed at ridiculous hours just like everyone else… only the next day I had to be punished for it, needing to restrict again and in constant panic the whole time.

I had moments where it felt like a big shift in my mind-set and days of feeling free. But I had experienced this many times now, in many admissions, so it did not have the same euphoria and hope attached to it, I just appreciated the actual moment.

A positive was that I was a lot closer to home so I had more visitors from my incredibly supportive friends and family. I remember a rainy day when my Mum came to visit me on her own and we stayed in playing games and talking all afternoon, which would never have happened before. It meant so much to our relationship after the strain it had taken with my illness.

There were other positive sides to The Priory and at times they did show signs of helping me. For instance, I was able to begin eating more independently by moving from the dining room within the ward, to our own section in the main dining room, to finally eating in the main hospital unsupervised. When visitors came, I could eat with them which was a huge step for us all. However, when my sister came for dinner one day, we had Red Velvet cake for dessert, and it was an excessively big slice. I was adamant that I could not eat it, but she sat with me through the tears and did not leave until she convinced me to do so, taking two hours. I remember her telling me it was red from beetroot, so really, it was healthy. When I finished it, she giggled and said, "as if, it is red food dye!" It did make me laugh too, slightly diffusing the situation.

I ate it to make her proud, I could not let her down. But when she left, I was left with "Rex" and I could not cope. I broke down and paced the corridors for an hour until allowed into my room, where I smashed my head against a wall so hard that I blacked out. I had to be punished.

I was also able to finally start exercising with a personal trainer in the hospital, but he was quite intense and mainly into boxing as he was the trainer for all of the wards where this kind of exercise may have been very beneficial. I don't think he quite understood the relationship someone with anorexia has with exercise and I got quite a full workout! This pleased "Rex" but I was naturally into this kind of sport as well and the joy it gave me.

It was close to beautiful Richmond Park for when I could go out freely, but this then became a trap for me as it is enormous, so I would walk from one end to the other which would take a few hours. "Rex" always took these opportunities and luxuries from me.

Then there was the internal yard with table tennis, giant chess and a relaxation section, which I never found myself in. The grounds were beautiful which helped on the days when we were allowed to go outside for therapy groups in the summer and sit on the grass.

A few members of staff really helped me and had great character, they were a lot of fun and this helped more than therapy sometimes. At the end of my admission, I remember calling them into my room to show them my safe where all my belongings should have been, but instead I had a stash of sweets, chocolate and caffeinated coffee! They were in such shock but laughed so much and then sat on my bed with me to share them, it spoke volumes.

But unfortunately there were also the members of staff who made life a living nightmare and were seemingly "power crazy" with enjoying their authority over us.

There was a time when we begged to be allowed to do a therapy group outside as it was a nice day, and I was at a healthy weight as were others. Eventually she gave in to let us have this fresh air but quickly and very sternly said, "but nobody is to stand up, if I see anyone stand up even once, we all go back inside right away."

I vividly remember one particular member of staff who was an authoritative male and would stand on top of the stairs overlooking the lounge with such an intimidating stance. He was waiting for one of us to move and would immediately shout "sit down" if you got up for a second, and if you were seen to get up too many times, he would threaten to give you a supplement of the build-up shake for doing too much exercise.

It made me feel panicked and trapped with no control over even moving my own body or having air.

They seemed to try and test your limits, but not in a helpful way. There was a time when another patient and I were eating together in the main dining room when we were further into recovery and doing really well. Out of nowhere they decided we had to go back to eat upstairs with those at the very beginning and with many difficult behaviours! We were so angry and they told us it was because we were under serving ourselves, but we served our food from the trolley for our ward with staff watching. They then said it was because we were sneaking food from the main dining room. It was a contradiction with the reasons being that we were restricting but also having too much. It was based on when we had once got salad from the buffet at the front when our meal was dry quiche and plain couscous with no colour or sign of a vegetable. Their final reason was that they decided we were eating too quickly which must be because we were wanting to go back upstairs to exercise while there were no staff there. Their evidence for this was because my weight had maintained for a week and not increased.

Another event that made no sense except for trying to create a reaction, was when I was close to my target weight and had gained 300g in a week, they insisted I needed an extra snack in my diet. That was evidently going to trigger my mind and was completely unnecessary. There was no way for them to justify it, but I had no control and had to do as they said, though I put up a fight as it seemed to be what they wanted. Drama. Tantrums. Screaming. Did it make their day more enjoyable and exciting?

I had become quite stubborn through my admission and so I retaliated by saying, *"I'll be refusing that snack tomorrow, then be given supplement which I'll also refuse, then you'll stop me going on walk or doing any activities, so I'll make a point and do a full body workout in the lounge until you give me back my freedom."*

A shocking event was when I became very anxious when I had not used all of the butter in the little pot for my toast when eating unsupervised. This was quite the opposite to those with an eating disorder and normally anxiety came from being made to use it all. But I felt incomplete, and this trait carried on for years, I felt nervous and on edge to leave anything on my plate. I believe it was from years of feeling punished when I did not finish things. So when I became quite physically and emotionally anxious with the unfinished pot of butter, the staff just gave me medication to calm me down. They did not talk to me about what was going on in my mind or find out what may have been the trigger, they just gave me sedative drugs. I was then still allowed to go out! I felt quite "out of it" with the suppressed anxiety and the medication, so I walked back and forth not knowing where to go, and just walked and walked and walked for four hours.

It came to a point where my Dad had to come up to sort things out as it was becoming ridiculous and more damaging. They were not letting me go outside for my one car park walk, I cannot remember the reason, but it was not valid. Being stuck inside all day around such chaos meant these moments of air were invaluable so I had a huge breakdown, screaming to let me out. My Dad arrived but it was too late, I had become some kind of demon. I started slamming doors, throwing things all around the ward and kicked the metal bin so hard that it dented it and went flying. I remember the shock on my Dad's face as he stood at the end of the corridor watching someone who was not their daughter, or even close.

Another time when I was eating in main dining room, I suddenly felt very claustrophobic and needed to get out, my head was screaming *"run"*, *"get out"*, *"they want to hurt you"*. With all that had happened, it was no surprise that I believed my mind and so I ran.

I got as far as the main reception before someone hit the alarms that go off around the hospital to call any free member of staff from any ward to come out and get you. I kept running. I got to the main entrance of the hospital grounds where I was then restrained by five people and to my utter amusement now, right underneath the sign "The Priory"!

My illness had become even more complex, I had many battles within my mind now and was riddled with demons. I understand the difficult position for everyone around me as this happened, it cannot have been easy. But it seemed to me that as I became healthier and began living with a bit more normality such as walking places for leisure, participating in sport or wanting a salad as opposed to a pie, people around me could not see past "Rex" anymore and would assume it was my illness. We would constantly argue over it and it became so stressful to make them believe me when it was me being just human, though again, after years and years of relapsing and deception, could I blame them? I needed to heal myself as well as others and all our relationships, so much had been destroyed.

I had become so self-involved and indulgent in my illness and with this, so had my friends and family, it is no wonder they had to distance from me, or they would go insane too. A friend finally had to tell me the truth and make me see this, it cannot have been easy and really took true friendship. She said I turned everything onto me and my illness, when she needed support when one of our other friends was really ill, I turned it to me. When she came over to see me, I would just care about when I could walk the dog and eating my dinner at the exact right time with no focus or thanks for her at all. *"I'm so glad she told me this as it makes me even more angry at the illness, I take responsibility for it and will change these controlling ways. Though I wish that my overdose was successful or I did not drink that charcoal, it would have been better for everyone. I don't feel suicidal now and would not do anything, but I wish it worked so I did not have to go through all this never-ending pain. I thought recovery would make me and everyone else happy, but it just seems to have brought a whole new kind of misery."*

I was at my target weight and a "healthy" BMI, so was I not now meant to feel better and life to be miraculously lovely again? I felt alone and frightened. I had all the rules in my head of activity, food and weight but this was no longer physically seen. I hit the gym hard, I did three laps of walking around the block and played table tennis into the evening. I was seen as healthy now, so I was allowed to do anything. It seemed to have gone from one extreme to another from too many rules and rigidity to nothing.

Things were already slipping at home on the weekends. I was restricting calories and feeling the awfully familiar sense of cold when under-nourished and forcing myself to be active despite feeling exhausted. I was comparing myself to everyone at work and to my Mum at home. Life was stressful for everyone when I got so angry and frustrated at my Mum, I feel guilty for how miserable I made everyone with this, but it was a huge trigger for my illness, it loved ruining my other relationships. We therefore decided that when I was discharged, I would live elsewhere in a house share. I had moved back with my parents after every admission and it ended up in destruction, so there was nothing to lose in trying something else.

After my final review, it was decided I would stay until the house share was available and then I would be sent on my way to face the world again.

I had started to come off some of my medication for anxiety and depression before being discharged and the withdrawal symptoms from these were so intense.

On my weekend leave, I felt unwell at work and had to go home, for me at this stage to give up a day of activity outside with distractions meant I felt *seriously* bad. I was getting heart palpitations, pins and needles and Mum said my pulse was irregular. I felt so sick and nauseous, physically unable to eat much this time but this soon becoming a great excuse for my anorexia as well.

Laying on the sofa, I soon felt lazy and needed to be punished for going home from work, so I walked to my sisters to help her move to a new house and felt so horrendous I wanted to collapse in the street and cry. *"But no, I must push myself."*

Luckily my Mum was a paramedic, as a patient should be monitored closely when coming off such high doses of medication, and I do not believe I should have gone home for the weekend. I wanted to put on a brave face when going back to the hospital because I was scared that they would put me back on the medication if I told them my reaction or stop my activities while coming off of them. But on my way back, I felt so awful both physically and mentally, so I called them to tell them I was worried and did not feel ok. When I arrived at the hospital, they searched my bags and took my shower curtain away so that I could not kill myself. That was all.

I wrote, *"I feel erratic, it is scary and confusing. This morning I woke up so early and just did not feel right, I felt panicked and just wanted to cry."*

And that was the last entry in my diary, I did not write any more.

12

A Scientific Case Study

All I know is another relapse began. Despite having the job I loved, a relationship, a good social circle, family life and being back on my university course. Again I ask, why?

What do we do this time? We had tried all the clinics and forms of therapy from the other relapses. So do we wait for my physical health to decline until forced to go back into a re-feeding hospital?

My Dad's friend called him, someone he did not speak to on a regular basis or who had much involvement with my illness, he just knew we were battling. He caught a snippet on the radio about a study that needed participants, he took notice and thought of me. It was one of the first studies to test Transcranial Magnetic Stimulation (TMS) as a possible form of treatment for chronic Anorexia Nervosa. The Tiara study.

My parents hesitantly told me, wondering how I would react. I was still determined and desperate to get better, so to their delight I e-mailed my application straight away. I had a reply the next morning saying I was the perfect candidate and that the study was starting in a couple of weeks. The applications which had been in process for a couple of years were about to close and some had been waiting all those years for it to start… dare I say I was lucky?

We were particularly excited about this trial as at the very beginning of my illness we found research about damage to the insular cortex within the brain being a cause of my anorexia. Since my illness began after suffering from hypoxia and I failed to recover no matter how hard we tried, we knew it had to be something within my brain chemistry that needed treating like any physical illness. When we had told doctors about this, they would not listen to us. Finally it had been found, what we knew all along, potential proof and ultimately a potential cure.

The study was in Kings College, so I travelled to London every day for five weeks. Though the actual treatment was fairly quick, taking no more than thirty minutes, it took most of my day to take four trains there and four trains back.

I had an initial assessment with a questionnaire, interview, various computer tasks and then an enduring MRI scan, where I had to complete tasks but then just stare at a white cross without being allowed to fall asleep! These lasted for hours and I had one at the beginning and another at the end of the trial.

After the assessments, the participants were split into two groups, some receiving the real treatment and some in the "placebo" group. It was a double-blind study so neither the participants nor the scientists administering the treatment knew what group we were in, though each group went through the same procedures.

I had electrodes attached to my head and between my index finger and thumb, they then placed a large magnet to my head, and I could see my brain on a screen. They kept administering the shockwaves to find the correct part of the brain, which they knew when my thumb twitched. It was a very strange sensation and shows how clever the mind is and how much it controls our whole being.

The treatment lasted for twenty minutes where they would stimulate my brain with electromagnetic pulsing for five seconds and then rest for fifty-five seconds. When reading about TMS now and further research into it, you will find it says, "pain free", but I found it incredibly painful, it was an indescribable type of pain, very sharp and deep within my brain. At the time I did not know this was abnormal and I would call my parents before going in because I was so scared of going through that pain again, and knowing it was coming was horrible!

I was just praying that I was a part of the real group so that it was all worth it.

At first it felt proactive with a potential ray of hope and to be a part of something that could help others. I also enjoyed travelling and being in London, after hospital admissions this was a huge sense of freedom.

But halfway through it changed for me. I remember sitting there in the treatment and looking at the electrode attached to my hand, looking at my brain on the screen and waiting for the painful pulses. Is this what my life had become? Just a scientific subject.

I became incredibly depressed. I was no longer hearing "Rex", but just falling into a deeper and darker hole each day.

I have spoken about the first overdose I took which was a cry for help. I have spoken of the second overdose I took to end my life, but with a glimmer of wanting to live and just about being saved. This time, I was going. There was not the impulse or adrenaline attached like before, I was calm and matter of fact in my mind about what I wanted.

However, I wanted to make a difference to the world before I went, have a reason to have been on this earth other than causing pain and suffering to myself and everyone around me, so I decided I would complete the study first.

It was not easy, and I vividly remember each day standing at the train station with my headphones on, listening to the James Arthur album "Recovery" so loudly and having to walk away from the platform when a train was going by that was not stopping because I did not trust myself. I often rang the Samaritans helpline who really were my saviours, they were incredibly helpful in keeping me going each day, to keep me going until the end of the study.

I planned my suicide while travelling to and from the treatment. On the last week of the study, I wrote the letter to my parents.

I went in on the last day of the trial to do the tasks I did at the beginning, for them to collect the data they needed and be on my way. My job here was done.

I wanted a final night to just lay and to feel nothing. Now I knew it was going to come to an end, the war inside me had stopped for the first time in years and I wanted to feel that unfamiliar sense of calm as my last memory.

There were no emotions of any sort and that is how I knew it was certain and what I wanted. My parents would understand, I was not sure if my sisters would, nor my friends, but after the relentless years of fighting and suffering, perhaps they would also see it as a relief for everyone.

I woke up the next morning in the same way, with an emptiness that is something I cannot explain. I had written a letter to my parents; they could explain to others.

It was a cold day and I went to open the front door to leave my flat for the last time. As I reached for the handle, there was a bumblebee on it which then flew at me. My senses and human instinct came back, and I moved away while flapping at the bee. It was this moment that not only saved my life, but completely changed it forever.

I do not know what happened. I am a very scientific person, agnostic, but also open minded about the spiritual life. I was very close to my Irish Grandma who would have been so helpful with my illness but had sadly passed away from cancer. I remembered being in awe when she would save bumblebees from spiders' webs and setting them free. She was not afraid and believed they could be saved when others would have turned away thinking it was their time, the circle of life.

She did not believe it was my time, she saved me.

I believe it gave me that human instinct back as I jumped and began flapping like most do at bumblebees and wasps flying around, and that this initiated the new neuropaths ways and my new brain chemistry.

I still left that door, but I went to the tattoo parlour to get a bumblebee on my arm, where I would promise to never lose hope in myself again. As I walked in, "You Are Not Alone" by Michael Jackson began playing.

I called my parents and asked if I could go over in the evening, that it was important. I brought a lot of wine with me as I told them everything and read them their letter.

They believed me, they genuinely believed that my mind was different now and that I was going to be ok. They did not feel they had to admit me to hospital or watch over me intensely, we somehow knew that I was going to recover.

It was not like in the movies where I suddenly smiled and danced my way through every day, it was still tough, and I had a lot to comprehend and work on. We all had a lot of healing to do. But from that day I never looked back and after a couple of years, I found peace in a full recovery, free of "Rex" and had won the war.

Three months later, I went back to Kings College to find out which treatment group I was in.

I had received the real treatment of TMS.

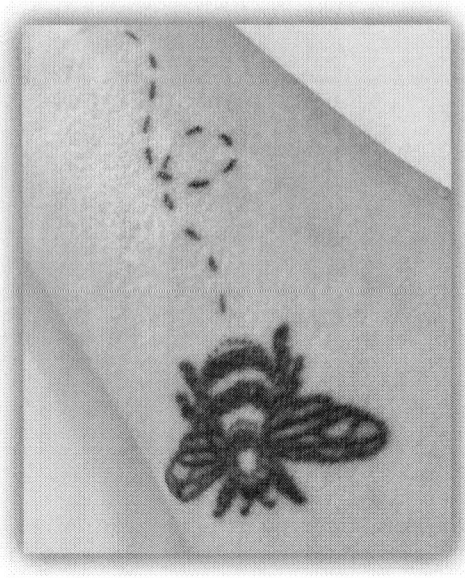

MUM'S EXPERIENCE

Our roller coaster ride of emotions started the day Rachael told us she was suffering from Anorexia nervosa at the age of 16. Through everyone's eyes it was a matter of telling us to make her eat, through our eyes it was trying to understand where we begin and what we can do to help her through the trauma of what Rachael was feeling mentally.

It was a far cry from what she was dealing with, the dark places she was leading to, Rachael became shut off to the world and even her family.

I remember the day that I took Rachael shopping to buy a dress for the biggest party of our lives, I feared seeing her in the dresses she tried on, the bones that stuck out, the arms the size of broomstick handles. I told her she looked beautiful, she was within, but the anorexia took her physical beauty away. This was the beginning of her 10-year battle.

We were afraid of going into her bedroom in the mornings, scared that she was no longer with us. Watching her curled up in a chair, her tiny frame pale and weak. The battle to stop her going out for walks, listening out for secret exercising or hidden food that we encouraged her to eat. The small amount of food that was being offered to her that she found so traumatised to eat.

We supported her to a funeral of a friend of hers who died from the illness and the shock of seeing all the other friends suffering from anorexia nervosa, wondering who will be next? Hoping it will be one of them and not my daughter and the guilt I felt thinking that way.

I saw a documentary on television about a place in Norwich treating people with anorexia nervosa, I contacted them in the hope of taking Rachael in. It took four hours to get there, just to get a consultation.

With the consultant, they accepted her but not for another week. Our journey back the following week was harrowing, Rachael had slipped into further decline, we were not sure if she was going to make it as she lay in the back seat of the car, very weak, no energy to even talk.

I had sleepless nights thinking the end of her journey was nearing, I was in turmoil wanting to ask her if she wanted burial or cremation, but I could not bring myself to ask her, it is something no parent should ever have to do.

DAD'S EXPERIENCE

When Rachael first admitted to having Anorexia nervosa, I really didn't have a clue what we were in store for, in fact I really didn't have a clue about anything related to it, I had that standard public misconception that any sufferer was doing it to themselves, they just wanted to look like the catwalk models in the media, no matter how much Rachael and her mother explained it to me, I just couldn't grasp it, it wasn't logical and therefore didn't "equate".

Then I saw a play called "Mess" by Caroline Horton, that changed my perception completely, in summary, Caroline suffered from Anorexia and portrays the illness as "voices" and "demons" in your head, constantly shouting at you, constantly driving you further and further downhill and into their grip, the sufferer has no control and the friends and family around you also get driven into helpless despair, the play has humour and despair, all I had was tears.

I was not going to let that happen to Rachael and to us, I had to find an answer, I looked into everything I could find.

This was in 2013, the BBC news page stated:

"Anorexia is recognised as the deadliest of all psychiatric illnesses, killing more people than alcohol and drug addiction and depression.

The outcome for patients remains extremely poor - only half the people who get it will recover.

New understanding of the disease is coming from research led by Prof Lask, who set up the eating disorders unit at Great Ormond Street Hospital.

Prof Lask believes one problem is that treatment focuses on restoring weight and not tackling the underlying issues:

"The focus is so much on re-feeding and weight restoration."

"We are struggling with the idea that once their weight is restored, they're cured. It is nonsense. They are not at all," he says."

His team have been researching a tiny part of the brain, the insula, which photo imaging technology shows to be underactive in people with anorexia.

For the next 10 years we as a family spoke to every source we could find, showing them further research in to the above, begging for help, just trying to find someone who would listen and understand, we proved that Hypoxia which Rachael suffered from triggers the distortion of the insula cortex, surely if that were the cause then someone could find the solution?

10 years of battling for help, 10 years of tearing Rachael, her family and friends apart, 10 years of the most horrible mental torture for us as parents, how we got through this I really do not know.

We did, we refused to accept the word "no", it affected every aspect of our lives, work, family and friends, it became all consuming, it is frightening how little help and understanding there is about this most horrible of illnesses, frightening how you have to fight and beg for help to keep your child alive. As a unit – despite many fractious times – we stuck together and supported each other, without our refusal to give in Rachael would not be here today giving back to so many people in the hope that one day there will be more places to get help, more treatments to address the many different facets of the illness.

Anorexia is a very broad word, there is no one type, there is no one cure, more treatments need to view anorexia as a mental rather than a physical condition and understand that the restriction on food is *the* major symptom of a mental illness and not the illness itself.

EPILOGUE

We do not have direct evidence that Transcranial Magnetic Stimulation was the reason I found a full recovery, but it was undoubtedly a significant piece of the puzzle.

Since recovery, I suffer side effects from what my body was put through, one of which being an inability to live in cold temperatures and I therefore had to move to warmer climates away from my family under medical instruction to do so. This was difficult to comprehend having finally found a mental recovery which had taken me from friends and family so many times, for so many years. However, it brought me to live in Malta where I have found a life I never thought possible, where I am truly happy.

Though facing many battles along the way, I never found myself at war with my mind again or using self-destructive coping mechanisms, which assured us that a full recovery had truly been found.

We may never know what exactly caused my physical condition with a medical history of such complexity. The hypoxia at the beginning, the severe malnourishment, the overdoses of medication, the blood infection from Ghana, the TMS treatment itself.

Though enduring and debilitating at times with severe physical pain, I will live on with a smile because nothing will cause me as much pain as Rex did.

I was incredibly lucky to survive, against medical odds on more than one occasion. Alice was just two weeks older than me, and we had planned that we would go to Disneyland Paris for our 25th birthdays, as this opened the year we were born. She did not make it, she passed away age 23.

The devastation remains raw in my heart, for me and her family, this never lessens. I still went to Disneyland Paris, healthy and recovered as I promised I would and celebrated for us both.

I lost many along the way, the sheer reality of mental health illness, the power of it. This is the reason I tell my story with such honesty and endeavour to help others, to use my survival as a gift to stop us from losing any more souls to these demons.

ACKNOWLEDGMENTS

It goes without saying to thank my family, friends and medical teams for keeping me alive, bringing me back to life and allowing me to find a full recovery. The true heroes deserve mention by name, Chris Hollwey and Patrick Hollwey, my devoted parents.

Thank you to my sisters, Amanda and Kim, for all your support to both myself and Mum and Dad. You are the inspirations for your strength while surrounded by this seemingly endless battle and continuing to visit me in all the hospitals with so much love and care.

Thank you to everyone who supported me, listened to me and allowed me to cry when reading, remembering and writing about the traumatic events.

Thank you for the overwhelming support in releasing this book, with it becoming so daunting at times that I felt I could not do it. We can do anything as a team.

Thank you to Infinity Publishing for their understanding in the meaning of this book and supporting me through the journey from beginning to end.

To those going through mental illness or caring for someone enduring a mental illness, I give you all my love and strength to keep going, to keep fighting and to win the war against your mind.

Manufactured by Amazon.com.au
Sydney, New South Wales, Australia